WORDSWORTH CLASSICS
OF WORLD LITERATURE

General Editor: Tom Griffith

THREE THEBAN PLAYS

To Ben-in-Fiction
with affection

Jamey Hecht

Hanukah 2005

Sophocles
Three Theban Plays

ANTIGONE

OEDIPUS THE TYRANT

OEDIPUS AT COLONUS

*Translated, with an Introduction
and Notes, by*

JAMEY HECHT

WORDSWORTH CLASSICS
OF WORLD LITERATURE

This edition published 2004 by Wordsworth Editions Limited
8B East Street, Ware, Hertfordshire SG12 9HJ

ISBN 1 84022 144 5

This edition © Wordsworth Editions Limited 2004
Introduction, Text and Notes © Jamey Hecht 2004

Wordsworth® is a registered trademark of
Wordsworth Editions Limited

Typeset by Antony Gray
Printed and bound in Great Britain by
Mackays of Chatham, Chatham, Kent

CONTENTS

Introduction   VII

Note on the Translation   XXIII

Suggestions for Further Reading   XXVI

First Performance Note on Antigone   XXVIII

ANTIGONE   I

OEDIPUS THE TYRANT   49

OEDIPUS AT COLONUS   107

Notes   173

INTRODUCTION

Tragic Wisdom

Greek tragedy is a kind of scripture that teaches us by showing, not telling, what we need to know. I call it a scripture because it is a religious discourse about human beings and their relationships to the divine realm of abundance and to the material world of scarcity. But it is also drama, a scripted matrix of interpersonal words and actions, as human and social as any conversation in the audience. Like all drama, tragedy is about individuals, but it also speaks to public life – Thebes and Athens and Corinth are not just crowded places but living societies with their own crises, wounds, and needs. Oedipus himself is a gifted man, endowed with an intellectual power that exposes him to special dangers. But he is also the Everyman that Freud made him. Though most people are spared the crimes of patricide and incest, and though psychoanalysis may have been wrong to posit a repressed yearning for them in every heart, it remains permanently true that nobody is in complete control of his own destiny. Just as we, the audience, can read the very script which the characters must live out, so the gods can read the fates which *we* must live out. Tragedy puts us (for once!) in the divine position of the invulnerable spectator, free to experience a safe terror as we identify with the endangered hero; free to feel a guarded pity for him insofar as we enjoy our blessed distance from his ruin.

Austere as it is, the art of Sophocles comes closer to life than any treatise on ethics could. It is free of precepts and instruction; within it, only experience teaches. Indeed, the work of growing up and old has in common with these tragedies the power to disclose necessary knowledge without the distortions that come with direct expression. As Oedipus learns, direct expression doesn't work anyway: he and Laius are each given clear oracles which they cannot successfully exploit. Apollo is not silent, but mortal persons lack his divine leverage upon their own affairs; without it, they can't use what they've been told. Any person, couple, family, or nation that has ever disregarded a prescient warning will recognise the exquisitely human agony of the tragic hero and his people.

It was Nietzsche who found life in this world so unjust and horrific that it 'could only be justified as an aesthetic phenomenon.' For him, Greek tragedy showed how the most grievous dilemmas and disasters have a wild beauty which only suffering reveals. There is a dangerous truth to this Nietzschean idea, because a misreading might allow interested opportunists to claim that *all* pain can be regarded as tragically beautiful, including whatever they or their leaders may choose to inflict. But tragedy is a picture of human suffering whose meaning inheres in its absolute inevitability; nothing could be more different from the sadist's licence to deliberate cruelty.* Apollo destroys Oedipus: not the Sphinx, not Creon, not some invading army. In Homeric epic, Apollo physically strikes Patroclus between the shoulder blades, and soon the man dies in battle. In Sophoclean tragedy, the god wields the man's own nature as the instrument of his destruction. Teiresias warns 'Apollo is enough,' and in his eventual agony Oedipus combines this with his own responsibility:

CHORUS

    O you who have done terrible things,
    How did you endure the breaking of your eyes?
    Which of the Gods had set you on?

OEDIPUS

    It was Apollo! Apollo, O my friends –
    That brought my wicked sufferings to pass;
    But no one struck my eyes
    But I myself in desperation.

---

* When Himmler wrote in his diary 'We were forced to come to the grim decision that this people must be made to disappear from the face of the earth,' he was pretending to overcome a tragic dilemma. In reality, his story was a banal melodrama, devoid of the moral complexity and

The god creates the conditions for the crimes which the man commits; then the man, by way of his noble character, punishes himself. This passage is special because it repeats Homeric motifs – the question 'which of the Gods,' followed by the answer 'Apollo,' comes from the opening of the *Iliad*, and the image of a blinded man who attributes his mutilation to 'No one' comes from the Cyclops episode in the *Odyssey*. But the ethical structure is distinctly Sophoclean. In *Antigone*, the tyrant Creon issues an edict that criminalises pious acts which the heroine then performs, through her noble character; she opts for the punishment when she commits the crime, and makes no effort to avoid capture. Near the end, she tells Ismene that 'I chose to die'; but a little later she says Hades is leading her to the banks of the river Acheron, then says that Creon is leading her captive. The god, the self, and the other are brought into a special, disastrous kind of contact that irreversibly changes the people without changing the god at all.

In *Oedipus the Tyrant*, we're told of Laius that 'fate drove down into his power,' but we also hear Oedipus describe the stick-fight that killed the man. In *Antigone*, the ruined Creon says 'the God struck down into my head.' But in the same speech he takes the personal and human responsibility we recognise from the protagonists of the other plays: 'The blame of it can never move / And be affixed to some man's guilt, away from mine! / It was I . . .' It is crucial that the person at the centre of the story be disposed to tragic suffering by his or her nature. What is irresistible is not simply the might of the god, nor the epistemic traps of logical entailment that comprise the plot; it is the performed fact of the person's life as he or she lives it. The truth here disappears if we hide it in the word 'character'; nobility is not some constraint that forces Oedipus to wound himself, Antigone to break a bad law, Creon to keep his word at all costs. Nor is it a magical property resting on a shelf in the mind until the circumstances warrant its use. It is an ethically strong moment that becomes aesthetically compelling when viewed from the safety of the amphitheatre or

personal cost that beset a figure like Creon. Here was Himmler's next sentence: 'We have tackled and carried it through without our men and our leaders suffering any damage in their minds and souls.'

the library. Tragic decisions are made at the peril of one's own moral life. The willingness to endure meaningful suffering – no matter how futile – is the only route to the salvation (literally, 'saving') of that moral life without which meaning is impossible.

Origins: Dionysus

Whatever we mean by 'ancient Greek religion,' it wasn't organised around a written text or a central holy site. Neither a private devotional practice nor a doctrinal enterprise with expansive, world-dominating ambitions, it was a wide range of local and pan-Hellenic cults, articulated in a common stock of stories (myths) and a diverse array of sacrificial rites, divinatory procedures, prayers, and social-economic pieties. Terms like 'Hinduism', 'Sufism', and 'Shinto' share this quality of necessary convenience at the expense of explanatory rigour; each is just a point of departure for a more demanding survey of the cultural plethora it denotes. While historical evolution tends to codify and homogenise every cultural formation, the formative period generally bristles with variation, syncretism, and a fertile cross-pollination that makes the beginnings more difficult for historians to extrapolate.

Theatre emerges in the Western world in the mid-sixth century BCE, when Athenian religion undergoes one of its many transformations. Although the origins of drama have fascinated scholars for centuries, our understanding of this mystery is likely to remain permanently incomplete. The starting point is a god, Dionysus, whose worship was long thought to have come into Greece from outside, somewhere in the Eastern regions that are now Syria and Turkey, perhaps by way of Thrace. While this god has special relevance to several different domains of Greek cultural life, Dionysus is most fundamentally the god of wine. He may have gained a reputation for Eastern origins because of the wine trade from Phoenicia to Greece ('Phoinikos' is a colour word that means anything from red to purple – the colours of grapes and of the various dyes for which that region was famous).

This tradition of a non-Greek origin for Dionysus has recently been complicated by the discovery of what seems to be a very ancient Greek form of his name inscribed on two tablets from the Mycenaean period, one from Pylos and one from Khania on the island of Crete. Greek culture begins around 1650 BCE with the permanent Mycenaean domination of that island, followed by the successful military expedition against Troy that probably took place around 1185 and which Homer immortalised in the *Iliad*. Our knowledge of the Mycenaeans rests largely on the happy fact that they left a record of the economic basis of their civilisation. While that record is mostly limited to the non-literary archives of the great palaces that dominated Mycenaean society, it does contain small traces of the larger cultural picture, including the names of the most ancient Greek divinities like Zeus, Hera, Poseidon, and Athena. Still, as Robert Drews has argued, the Greeks are themselves a people or peoples who migrated into the Aegean region as part of the Indo-European expansion during the second millennium BCE. So the pantheon can be rather crudely described as a combination of two classes: gods who were common to the entire Indo-European family that spread over a vast area, to Ireland in the west and India in the east; and local, pre-Indo-European gods who were picked up by proto-Greek migrants en route to the Aegean and during the process of eventual settlement. Neither of these fits with the idea of uniquely Greek origins for Dionysus nor for any other god.

But there's another sense in which Dionysus can be thought of as a stranger to the human world. Whereas other gods sometimes bring safety and assistance – as when Hermes gives Odysseus the antidote for Circe's destructive magic, or Ino brings him a veil that magically prevents drowning – Dionysus has a chaotic, boundary-breaking influence. He's the god of everything that threatens rational conscious choice: wine, religious ecstasy, orgiastic violence (other than war, of which Ares and Athena are the sponsors), orgiastic sex (other than the emotional attachments governed by Aphrodite and Eros), and the strange form of possession that constitutes theatre. His alternate name is Bacchus, and the *Baccheia* were a wilder form of his cult, fully available only to women: every other year, bands of female worshippers left the sane, rational, male precincts of human society and entered the savage, ecstatic, female and borderless realm of mountains and wilderness in a shared Dionysiac trance that made them *mainades*, 'madwomen'. The more civic forms of piety toward Dionysus were regulated in various seasonal festivals: the *Oschophoria*, a celebration of wine and vintnery with a procession that carried grapevines; the *Anthesteria*, a flower festival involving drink from various sacred vessels as well as singing and story; and the two dramatic festivals, the *Lenaea* and the Greater Dionysia. Worship of Dionysus seems to have involved countless forms of movement between categories, the stable borders of which are civilisation's most basic achievement: the female and the male gender roles, the demos (common people) and the aristocracy, the urban and the natural, the raw and the cooked. Building on the work of Claude Lévi-Strauss, structuralist interpreters of Greek tragedy such as Charles Segal have explored the way Sophocles contains the explosive energies liberated by this aspect of the Athenian psyche.

From various sources including Aristotle, it appears that the Dionysia began as a ritual dance performed by a chorus of fifty men moving in a circle; they spoke or sang a kind of poetry called dithyramb, probably in unison, punctuated by the speech or song of a single chorus leader. In 534 BCE, an historically real individual named Thespis *invented drama* by stepping out of the chorus – without ending or leaving its activity – and engaging it in dialogue. It was presumably this advent of *dialogue* that turned ritual into theatre, and not the mere addition of a new, separate stream of discourse *beside* the chorus. In talking to the chorus leader and his followers while remaining inside the symbolic frame of Dionysian sacred space, Thespis became an actor. Friedrich Nietzsche emphasised this continuity between the pre-thespian and the tragic phases of civic Dionysiac practice. He claimed that even before the supposed dialogic event of 534, dithyramb already involved the same kind of possession we associate with an actor possessed by a character: for Nietzsche, the fully entranced chorus leader entered the role of Dionysus.

Through the agency of an enlightened despot named Peisistratos, Thespis's innovation brought about a regular, annual competition in the dramatic art. Each year, three chosen poets submitted four works each – three tragedies and a 'satyr play', a brief comedy featuring lustful, drunken beast-men. A public official selected the competitors from a larger pool of applicants in an audition process held months in advance, and appointed a prosperous citizen to pay the costs of hiring and organising the chorus. We're accustomed to a form of theatre in which producers hope for a financial return on their investment, and audience members pay to be entertained on an evening of their own choosing. The ancient theatre was completely different in this regard. Just as the hero is both an individual and a figure for the whole society and ultimately for mankind in general, so the audience member is an individual social person who is also much more than that. Whatever the level of religiosity remaining to it in the fifth century, the festival of Dionysus was a profoundly civic occasion; it connected Athenians to one another and situated their political community in the cosmos at large. All male citizens (and probably their wives as well, though this remains controversial) came to the performance, and the society was just small enough that the enormous outdoor amphitheatre seems to have been adequate for the purpose – in his *Symposium*, Plato estimates an audience at thirty thousand. Christian Meier has described the problem–solving dimension of tragic drama, in which Athens grappled with otherwise intractable dilemmas of public affairs. In the Freudian tradition (unscientific, but always interesting), it makes sense to compare this political aspect of tragedy with the role of dreams in the psychic economy of each man or woman. What Freud called 'the dream-work' is a confrontation of issues for which the conscious, waking mind is ill-equipped. On this analogy, the person's rational mind corresponds to the rational debate pursued in the Ecclesia ('public assembly'), while the tragic consciousness does something like the dream-work of the culture that produces it. Christopher Gill and C. Fred Alford are among the scholars who make fruitful use of the psychoanalytic legacy in divergent ways.

Sophocles' Life

The most shocking fact about this greatest of playwrights is that his seven surviving works are all that remain of some 123 plays. Imagine finding that the First Folio were actually one seventeenth of Shakespeare's total output, and you have some emotional idea of the pathos in this loss. This is a fascinating story in its own right; and authors like Leo Deuel and Leighton D. Reynolds narrate the often thrilling anecdotes of textual destruction and discovery that have accumulated over the centuries.

In 480 BCE, Aeschylus fought in the Battle of Salamis against the

Persian invaders. Sophocles, born in about 496, danced in the boys' victory chorus organised to celebrate that battle. Selection for such a chorus was based partly on physical beauty; the young Sophocles had both natural graces and achievements, having won prizes for wrestling and music. One tradition, associated with a fourth century author called Aristoxenus, holds that the playwright's origins were modest, and that his father was a carpenter. But the other view, also supported by ancient sources, is that the skilled labour of Sophocles' father was part of a larger enterprise of which he may have been the head; say, a military supplier. In that case, his family were beneficiaries of the wealth that flourishing trade and tribute brought into Attica, wealth which grew as Athenian regional power expanded. But with that expansion came a terrible price in political integrity as the city's conduct of its external affairs turned increasingly imperial, cynical, and sometimes rapacious. Like Socrates (the philosopher of Plato's dialogues), Sophocles wrestles with the cultural identity crisis developing in Athens at the time of its greatest achievements. And unlike Plato, Sophocles viewed the unfolding, glorious ordeal of the fifth century from the viewpoint of a participant and, later, as a retrospective thinker who remembers.

In his first tragic competition at the Greater Dionysia of 468, Sophocles won first prize, all the more impressive because Aeschylus was also competing that year. A further twenty-three victories followed, eighteen in the Greater Dionysia and six (or as some sources have it, two) in the Lenaea. He won far more frequently than any other competitor, and whenever he did not win, he took second place. Nor was this the result of happy luck with a few judges; at twenty-eight years old, he was so popular that his first contest required unusual measures for the keeping of public order. As his prodigious artistic career advanced, the city prevailed upon him for public service, which he rendered faithfully. Athens was the dominant centre of the Delian League, a system of military alliances originally designed to ward off the threat of Persian aggression. It elected Sophocles to the post of Treasurer in 443 BCE, no small responsibility since the repository at Delos housed the annual tribute sent to Athens (in exchange for security guarantees) from Greek cities all over the Aegean. Two years later, Sophocles was chosen to serve as one of ten army generals, allegedly because of the political wisdom demonstrated in the recently produced *Antigone*. He fought at the battle of Samos, a difficult naval engagement in which Athens eventually prevailed. In keeping with the social nature of his genius, he enjoyed the friendship of the period's greatest statesman, Pericles, many of whose vexing moral questions seem to be reflected in the plays. Victor Ehrenberg was among the first scholars to investigate the implications of that friendship. He and others have suggested that Sophocles' insight into Pericles' character and career may have shaped the figure of King Oedipus; each considered himself a man of rare intelligence and fortitude whose passionate commitment could save a plague-afflicted city.

Toward the end of his life and after his death in 406, Sophocles came to be regarded with an admiration amounting to reverence. A profoundly religious person, he was honoured around the year 420 with the opportunity to share his house with the symbolic presence of the divine physician Asklepios. That hero-god's symbol was a living, sacred snake, which Sophocles formally received into his home, earning him the name *Dexios*, 'the Receiver'. Under that name, he was honoured by a hero-cult of his own after his death in 406 at the age of ninety. His longevity remains an important element of his image, partly because of an anecdote in Plato's *Republic* in which Sophocles is said to express relief that old age has freed him from the sexual appetites of the body. But more importantly, the playwright's almost incomparable powers of composition never failed him. His drama *Philoctetes* was produced in 409, when he was eighty-seven year old. It is among the world's deepest statements about suffering, loss, and forgiveness, comparable with the *Book of Job* and perhaps *King Lear*, but with very little else. His last play, *Oedipus at Colonus*, was produced by his grandson in the year 401.

Antigone

The dates of first theatrical production (and therefore, approximate dates of composition) for the three Theban plays are:

Antigone:	442–441
Oedipus the Tyrant:	429
Oedipus at Colonus:	401

But these three tragedies form a single story, since they are elaborations of a single system of myths that was centuries old in Sophocles' time (Oedipus is mentioned, for instance, in Homer's *Odyssey*). The events in the story flow this way:

1   *Oedipus the Tyrant*
2   *Oedipus at Colonus*
3   *Antigone*

Although the narrative action of *Antigone* happens *after* that of *Oedipus the Tyrant* and *Oedipus at Colonus*, it is often printed ahead of the other two because it was written first.

Oedipus leaves two sons, Eteocles and Polyneices. But the very opening scene of *Antigone* tells us that they have just died horribly, having killed each other in a civil war over the throne of Thebes. The male powers in Antigone's nuclear family are all gone. Her uncle Creon had been the 'General', a regent or custodian of the state during the youth of the two princes. Because of their deaths, he becomes king. Now, this is not the direct violation that Hamlet experiences when *his* uncle becomes king by murdering Hamlet's father, but Creon's ascension to the throne is a function of Antigone's bereavement. Having spent her youth nursing her blind father, she too comes into her own when these brothers die; it is as if her life finally begins. In the Athenian democracy and the legendary past which it imagines in tragic drama, women's political existence is never supposed to happen, and Antigone's defiance is explicitly treated as a violation of gender roles.

The story looks simple: Thebes suffers a civil war. Eteocles, the younger of the two princes, takes the throne, but Polyneices claims it and brings an army from Argos as his ally. Eteocles and the Thebans win, but the brothers kill one another in battle. Creon, their uncle, becomes king. His first act in office is the promulgation of an edict forbidding the burial of Polyneices, whose army had killed Theban soldiers and attacked the city's defences. Now the only surviving children of Oedipus are the dead men's sisters, Antigone and Ismene. Burying their kin is their sacred right and obligation, but the new king has just forbidden it on pain of death. Ismene chooses to survive and obey, while Antigone chooses to defy Creon and his law, well aware that she must lose her life in punishment. She makes a ritual burial over Polyneices and is apprehended. Creon interrogates her and dispatches her to an underground crypt for imprisonment and eventual death by starvation. Then he argues about Antigone's case with her fiancé – his own son Haemon – who claims to represent public opinion. That argument ends the relationship between father and son, and Creon never sees Haemon alive again. As the Chorus becomes increasingly anxious about Creon's conduct – which violates the demands of the gods by leaving Polyneices unburied, and by punishing Antigone – the prophet Teiresias arrives. In a frightening speech, he explains that pestilence, war, and death will follow from Creon's decisions. The king finally realises this, and frantically tries to prevent further harm, but he arrives at Antigone's tomb to find his son Haemon dead beside her body. When a messenger tells all this to Queen Eurydice, she kills herself in grief for her son. The messenger then meets Creon in the tomb and announces the queen's death. Though he remains alive, Creon is utterly ruined.

While everyone in the play suffers, Antigone and Creon are the two foci of a monumental ordeal which ultimately destroys them. While Antigone dies a physical death as the price for enacting her ethical identity, Creon lives to see his whole life shattered by his own mistakes. A speech of Haemon compares Creon to the unbending branch that breaks in the winter flood, while those that bend in the current are saved. The metaphor is directed at Creon, but it applies just as well to Antigone. Each is a rigidly passionate claimant to the right, driven by the conviction that he/she knows exactly what must be done. One difference, however, is that Antigone understands the cost of that rigidity before she makes her choice; Creon does not. Another difference is power: Antigone is physically helpless, but her only responsibility is to her family and the gods who govern family obligations. Creon has the full power of the state at his disposal, but he bears an equally absolute responsibility for its governance. His emotional loathing of the rebel Polyneices may be a major factor in his decision to forbid the burial, but his consciously avowed motivation is the need for moral coherence: if the king does not punish traitors, the whole society may disintegrate. Since a dead man can only be punished one way, Creon commits to it. Once he does so, his own notion of authority denies him any recourse, until it is too late for recourse.

Oedipus the Tyrant

Tragedy is not easy to appreciate. Even if one knows something about the ancient Greeks, has lived long enough to feel mortal, and cares about someone else enough to feel concerned about loss – even if one has achieved a healthy susceptibility to Sophocles' power – it is hard to let go of our more comfortable attitudes. Modern inheritors of Athenian democracy (in the various cultures which claim to espouse it) tend to grow up in an atmosphere of optimistic propaganda. The idea that hard work and education will always conduce toward a happy life is perhaps central to the teaching of humanities and social sciences in schools and universities on both sides of the Atlantic. Yet in these same classrooms people are encouraged to read Athenian tragedies in which the most zealous, gifted, public-minded persons are brought to grief and horror through the unwanted consequences of their own efforts. Modern society is stuck with the tragic drama, as the Church and its fellow monotheist institutions are stuck with the *Book of Job* and *Ecclesiastes*.

The plot of *Oedipus the Tyrant* is like a closed sculpture in logical space, a spellbinding mobius-strip of fate and decision that can't be resolved by human insight. Causality seems to flow in both directions, backward from a predicted future and forward from an irrevocable past. Because the action of the drama takes place on a single day (near the middle of Oedipus' life), the present is a turning pivot or hinge, that can neither be stopped nor controlled. True, the protagonist has a choice whether to press forward with his ultimately disastrous investigation, or leave well enough alone; but given the inner facts of his nature and the outer state of the city for whose welfare he is responsible, Oedipus has to press forward.

Laius, king of Thebes, receives a divine oracle from the shrine of Apollo stating that a son will kill him. When his wife Jocasta gives birth, Laius arranges for the infant boy to be killed instead. This can't be done directly, because infanticide is a religious crime. So the royal parents use a practice that was not rare in the ancient world: exposure. They send a servant to bring the infant Oedipus out to the slopes of the wild mountain Cithairon, there to be abandoned and exposed to the elements, his feet pinned together with a stake. A Corinthian shepherd finds the infant and rescues him out of pity, taking him to King Polybus of Corinth and his queen, Merope. They raise Oedipus as their own son, but when a drunken man calls him a 'counterfeit son' (i.e. adopted), he goes to Apollo's oracle at Delphi for information. There he hears the same oracle that had come to Laius: that Oedipus will kill his own father and beget children in a marriage with his mother. In a desperately determined effort to avoid this, he flees the only parents he knows – Polybus and Merope, of Corinth – and goes in search of some other life. Along the way, near a triple crossroads, he meets an old man with servants in a chariot. A fight ensues; Oedipus kills the old man and all the attendants but one. Oedipus travels on and, near the city of Thebes, meets with the Sphinx. She is a supernatural monster who poses her famous riddle to one man after another, killing them when they fail to solve it. Oedipus hits on the correct answer, and the Sphinx destroys herself. Having saved the city, he marries its widowed queen, Jocasta, and thereby becomes king. After several years of a successful reign, a plague breaks out. The action of the play begins at this point.

Showing the same courage and intelligence for which he has justly become famous, Oedipus resolves to find the source of the plague which is killing his people. He sends his brother-in-law, Creon, to the oracle of Apollo for information. Creon returns with the news that the plague comes from the presence of an unpunished murderer in their midst, the unknown killer of Laius. Now Oedipus pronounces a curse on the guilty one, whoever he is, and pledges to identify him. That investigation proceeds apace, until Oedipus realises that Laius was in fact the old man whom he killed in self-defence all those years ago. This is terrible enough, because the curse he invoked upon the murderer of Laius is now fallen on his own head – one more example of the king's unwitting self-destruction. But the radically unique horror of his fate begins to emerge when this first question (*who killed Laius?*) inexorably converges with the next question: *who am I?* As Teiresias points out, this is the riddle Oedipus cannot solve, despite the skill with riddles he demonstrated when he defeated the Sphinx.

The answer comes in the form of a traveller from Corinth, who announces Polybus' death. In a somewhat amazing coincidence, this Corinthian turns out to be the same shepherd who received the infant Oedipus from the man who first brought him to

Cithairon mountain on Laius' orders. An equally amazing co-incidence immediately follows: Oedipus sends for the sole survivor of his attack on Laius, and that man turns out to be this very messenger – the man who brought him to Cithairon for his death, and then, through pity, to Corinth for his life. All the elements of the emerging truth match Apollo's prediction. Having seen this, and having seen the naked body of his mother, he blinds himself with the pins that held her robe together. After a return to the stage and a piteous farewell to his daughters, Oedipus prepares to leave Thebes with Creon's eventual permission, and the play ends. When the mutilated Oedipus leaves Thebes, never to return, he is repeating the maiming and expulsion that followed his birth; in a sense, he is reborn in the truth, having lived a falsehood until then. He is also repeating his self-expulsion from Corinth, which was also a flight from royal status into homeless exile.

Although the complete riddle of the Sphinx does not appear in the play, we have the text from other sources, including a black-figure vase from the 520s: 'There is on earth a being two-footed, four-footed, and three-footed that has one name; and, of all creatures that move upon earth and in the heavens and in the sea, it alone changes its form. But when it goes propped on most feet, then is the swiftness in its limbs the weakest.' The name Oedipus has at least two derivations, of which the first comes from his terrible infancy: *oidôn tô pode*, 'with swollen feet'. Having his two feet pinned together makes of them a single, useless foot. The other derivation of Oedipus is a compound of *oida*, 'know', *pous*, 'foot'; he's the one who knows the riddle of the foot, yet he's the person to whom the riddle does not apply. The riddle's answer is, of course, man. But Oedipus never walked on two feet without the walking stick that makes a third 'foot' in the riddle.

Almost every line spoken by or about Oedipus in this drama has a double or even a triple meaning. The hero is only conscious of one meaning, beneath whose surface the bitter ironies of the other meanings are coursing. A reader can open the play anywhere and apply his or her knowledge of the text and its story to discover double meanings, some that appear instantly and others that dawn on the reader after years of acquaintance with the Sophoclean world.

Oedipus at Colonus

The dates of the plays are not known with certainty, but we do know that *Oedipus at Colonus* is the last of the plays. Sophocles died in 406, two years before the final defeat of Athens in the decades-long war with Sparta. The playwright, more than ninety years old, seems to create this play as a farewell to life – and to the city of Athens which he served and which nurtured and rewarded him. Although he experienced the tragedy of the Peloponnesian War and the breakdown of the cultural order that we associate with Classical Athens, he didn't live to see its awful collapse of 404. The first production of the *Colonus* was directed by the poet's grandson in 401. In the resolution of the play, Oedipus' burial is said to confer the blessings of victory and prosperity upon Athenian soil forever, though the audience knows all too well that this does not prove true. Though Sophocles may have seen the end coming for Athens, there is some historical pathos in the fact that it happened just after his death and just before, as it were, the first death of Oedipus to be performed on the Athenian stage at the Greater Dionysia.

There is meaning in the fact that *Antigone* comes first in Sophocles' writing life, but last in the narrative of the Theban plays. In 401 the audience of the playwright's last work had either heard, or heard about, the *Antigone* of forty years before. When the aged Oedipus and the young Antigone walk into the district of Colonus at the border of Athenian territory, a stranger comes and urges them to leave their position. They have wandered onto sacred ground, a holy grove dedicated to a group of terribly powerful goddesses called the Eumenides. Athenian elders are summoned, and they again tell Oedipus to stop what they see as the sacrilege of his remaining seated where he is. At that point Antigone urges her father to obey the local customs and do as they say. Here, then, is Antigone obeying a civic authority (in Athens) that is consistent with a religious sanction, just as in her own drama she had disobeyed one that wasn't (in Thebes). This is one of the many ways in which the two cities are opposites, with Thebes as the sick city of tyranny and unregulated violence, and Athens as the healthy city of political reason and a bright future.

In *Oedipus the Tyrant*, the hero began high up in the cosmos (an accomplished, gifted king) and ended as a beggar; here, the reverse occurs. Oedipus' guilt and its pollution were at the heart of his identity and his destiny then; but now, the guilt is resolved into its origins: we finally hear him explain that his patricide was done in self defence, and his incest was done in ignorance. The pollution is dispelled. This has more than one sufficient explanation. From the point of view of retributive justice, Oedipus was already punished severely, by his own hand, long ago. From the point of view of religious pollution, the *miasma* that made him an outcast from Thebes and the rest of the human community has been reversed: it is divinely ordained that whoever receives Oedipus will enjoy good fortune. This is not, however, an authorial squandering of the accumulated moral complexity of the story. Whereas the god at the end of the *Book of Job* simply blesses Job at the end of that story, returning sevenfold all that the poor man had lost, Oedipus has to bring his dying body into an unknown sacred place on his own decision. That entails an agonising scene of rejection in which two Theban claimants try, and fail, to keep him connected to his old life: Creon, who tries to force him back to Thebes, and his own son Polyneices, who tries to persuade him. Though the play ends with the emergence of the holy, this is not a *deus ex machina* that suddenly fixes it all. Oedipus' own development is outwardly manifest as the consummation of his death and the establishment of that local Athenian hero-cult which marks his greatness. What makes death painful for aged men and women is not regret, we are told, but unfinished business. When this exhausted old man dies at last, having resolved all his affairs that once seemed so utterly irredeemable, his body seems to disappear, as though the gods had simply removed him from the earth. The ending of the drama of his old age fulfills the ending of the drama of his youth:

> fixing our gaze
> Upon life's final day, we shall call no mortal happy,
> Until he cross the threshold of this life, free from pain.

NOTE ON THE TRANSLATION

Athenian tragedy is the recollection of a royal, legendary, distant past in the theatre of a civic, democratic present. The chorus speaks in an archaic, metrically grand idiom that evokes the enormous stakes for which the legendary principals are playing. We have a similar institution in our own culture, an institution called Shakespeare, in which post-modern American audiences and readers confront kings and queens thinking, feeling, and fighting in Elizabethan diction. Just as in Athenian tragedy, the height of the style conveys the nostalgia of the aristocracy, the cosmic terror and the irreversible spiritual risks that kings and their families inflict and suffer, and the deep and urgent sense that these poor beings on the stage are ourselves.

This is a verse translation because the original is verse. The translation is *blank verse* because that is the metre of high drama in English. My goal was a faithful rendering of the Greek into memorable English, showing as many of the logical structures of Sophoclean ideation and idiom as possible. Sophocles is rhetorically situated between the aristocratic declamation of Aeschylus and the more modern, conversational language of Euripides; moreover, the action of these plays concerns the affairs of royal persons and their families. Therefore I had to work in an English that would answer to the dignity of Sophocles' poetry, but remain accessible to a contemporary audience.

This required a high style, tuned to the peculiar urgency of ancient, royal, dramatic action. Like *Oedipus the Tyrant*, Shakespeare's *Henry V*, *Julius Caesar*, *Hamlet*, and *Coriolanus* are built of dialogue and soliloquy laden with all the conventions of sovereignty: entreaty, permission to speak, defiance, retort, forensic and deliberative speeches, the contribution of advice and its dismissal, the marvelling of the bystanders as the king succeeds or fails. Those speech-situations are bound to develop wherever a king rules: they are common to pre-democratic Athens and Elizabethan England. While modern American language might be interesting in an *adaptation* of Sophocles, this is a *translation*. Therefore it aspires to be Sophoclean, and it happens that Shakespeare is especially useful for this. There appear to be a number of matches between the grammar of Ancient Greek and late sixteenth century English. Greek employs, for example, the double disjunction — it says '*or* X *or* Y' rather than '*either* X *or* Y'; something English no longer does, but once did beautifully: 'My learned Lord, we pray you to proceed, / And justly and religiously unfold, / Why the Law Salique, that they have in France, / *Or should, or should not, bar us in our claim.' Henry V*, 1, 2. I believe I have a precedent like this one for every archaism I have used, and on the whole I have tried to translate as simply and as accurately as possible.

There is no danger of conflating the historically specific forms of governance and religion found in Ancient Athens (or Thebes) with those of 16th Century England: the text of Sophocles and the idiom of Shakespeare already possess a common stock of tropological and grammatical resources. By 'the idiom of Shakespeare' I do not mean, except in a few cases, that I have stolen phrases from the Bard; I mean that I've employed what Moses Hadas called 'moderate [rather than] extreme archaism' of an Elizabethan, and not a Victorian, type. I have laboured to let the Greek legal, political, mantic, and supplicatory institutions take up something like the emotional space they occupy in the Greek.

Accordingly, I have capitalized the nouns 'God' and 'the Gods' throughout (but not the adjectives 'godlike,' 'godly,' or 'godless'), although this is somewhat unconventional, because the convention arose in the context of a monotheist philology protecting its practitioners from blasphemy. The lowercase *g* at the beginning of 'the gods' immediately and unconsciously turns off whatever religious seriousness might otherwise be available to the reader's experience. A more Sophoclean alternative is to signify the majesty of the powers of Athenian religion by capitalizing the word (in both the singular and the plural), and a precedent can be found for this approach in Walter Otto's *The Homeric Gods*. The work of

Ruth Padel does a similar job, on more psychological grounds. All nouns are capitalized in German, so this typographical issue does not arise in Nietzsche's *Birth of Tragedy from the Spirit of Music*, but there is no mistaking the tone of Nietzsche's joyful seriousness about Apollo and Dionysus, a tone I find worthy of emulation.

Consider the judgment of Moses Hadas, in his 1967 introduction to Jebb's prose translation:

> A reader who attends to Sophocles as a monument in the history of the human spirit may find transparent prose a truer reflection than verse. But the prose must not be commonplace, as it may be for Euripides; *it must communicate the stately remoteness of the original.* The most carefully wrought prose version is that of Sir Richard Claverhouse Jebb (1841–1905), *which has the merit not only of extreme accuracy but also of maintaining a high formalism and dignity appropriate to Sophocles.* [my emphasis]

For this, Jebb quite logically employed a prose idiom without lineation, setting the choruses and the long speeches, or soliloquies, in paragraph form. But Jebb's prose is more poetic than the poetry of many mid-century translators. Professor Hadas did, in editing Jebb for the Bantam reprint, 'substitute moderate for extreme archaism . . . in cases where the modern reader might be puzzled', but on the whole he let Jebb's version stand, as a major statement of what this play sounds like when it 'maintains a high formalism and dignity appropriate to Sophocles'. Hadas continues:

> Jebb's device for lending dignity to a prose version of stately poetry was to use archaism in vocabulary, wordforms, word order – in a word, to emulate the English of the King James Bible.

This was no mere device: Jebb knew that when modern readers heard the language of William Tyndale and his late-Tudor and early Jacobean successors, they would be reminded of kingship, of religious crisis, of the persistence of the past in the present. In the language of the King James translators (whose Authorized Version remained overwhelmingly indebted to the solitary work of Tyndale), the authority and the peril of both the Biblical and the Elizabethan pasts cast their rhetorical spell on modernity. Shakespeare's idiom comes from the same phase of our language's development; in it, too, we can hear human speech ascend to prophetic heights.

I enjoyed the assistance of the following editions and commentaries:
　　Nicolas P. Gross's 1988 Bryn Mawr Commentary on *Antigone*;
　　Lewis Campbell and Evelyn Abbott's 1878 Oxford Clarendon
　　Oedipus at Colonus;
　　Richard Claverhouse Jebb's 1900 *Complete Works of Sophocles,
　　Texts and Fragments*;
　　Gilbert Rose's 1988 Bryn Mawr Commentary on *Oedipus at
　　Colonus;*
　　The Perseus Digital Library, Tufts University; Gregory
　　Crane, Editor in Chief.

The following people read portions of the manuscript and pro-
vided advice and encouragement: Seth Benardete, Frank Bidart,
Jack Collins, Jonathan Galassi, Tom Griffith, Rachel Hadas,
Eugene Hecht, Ali Hossaini, Stephen Klass, Fyodor Korzhukhin,
Julie Kunzie, Gregory McNamee, Gregory Nagy, Alan Shapiro,
and Alan Thomas. I also wish to thank Eugene Goodheart of
Brandeis University, who granted the tuition for my attendance at
the City University of New York's *Latin Greek Institute* in 1992.

SUGGESTIONS FOR FURTHER READING

Aeschylus, *Seven Against Thebes*

Frederick Ahl, *Sophocles' Oedipus: Evidence and Self-Conviction*,
　　Cornell University Press, 1991.

C. Fred Alford, *The Psychoanalytic Theory of Greek Tragedy*, Yale
　　University Press, 1992.

Jean Anouilh, *Antigone*

Seth Benardete, *Sacred Transgressions: A Reading of Sophocles'*
　　Antigone, St. Augustine's Press, 1999.

Walter Burkert, *Greek Religion*, Harvard University Press, 1987.

Rebecca Bushnell, *Prophesying Tragedy: Sign and Voice in
　　Sophocles' Theban Plays*, Cornell University Press, 1988.

Leo Deuel, *Testaments of Time: The Search for Lost Manuscripts and Records*, Knopf, 1965.

Robert Drews, *The Coming of the Greeks: Indo-European Conquests in the Aegean and the Near East*, Princeton University Press, 1988.

Robert Drews, *The End of the Bronze Age: Changes in Warfare and the Catastrophe ca. 1200 B.C.*, Princeton University Press, 1993.

Victor Ehrenberg, *Sophocles and Pericles*, Basil Blackwell, 1954.

Joseph Fontenrose, *The Delphic Oracle: Its Responses and Operations*, University of California Press, 1978.

Christopher Gill, *Personality in Greek Epic, Tragedy, and Philosophy: The Self in Dialogue*, Oxford University Press, 1996.

Christian Meier, *The Political Art of Greek Tragedy*, Johns Hopkins University Press, 1993.

Friedrich Nietzsche, *The Birth of Tragedy From the Spirit of Music*, originally published 1872.

Leighton D. Reynolds and N.G. Wilson, *Scribes and Scholars: A Guide to the Transmission of Greek and Latin Literature*, Oxford University Press, 1965.

Charles Segal, *Tragedy and Civilization: An Interpretation of Sophocles*, University of Oklahoma Press, 1981.

Charles Segal, *Oedipus Tyrannus: Tragic Heroism and the Limits of Knowledge*, Twayne, 1993.

Charles Segal, *Sophocles' Tragic World*, Harvard University Press, 1995.

William Shakespeare, *King Lear*

M. S. Silk and J. P. Stern, *Nietzsche on Tragedy*, Cambridge University Press, 1981.

Phillip Vellacott, *Sophocles and Oedipus*, University of Michigan Press, Ann Arbor, 1971.

Jean-Pierre Vernant and Pierre Vidal-Naquet, *Myth and Tragedy in Ancient Greece*, Zone Books 1988.

FIRST PERFORMANCE NOTE ON ANTIGONE

This translation of *Antigone* was first performed in the theatre at Chashama, on 42nd Street in NYC. Michael McCartney played the role of Creon; John Breen, Antigone; Jason Stevens, Teiresias; Jamey Hecht, Eurydice; Patrick Burch, Haemon; Dan Laughlin played the Page. *Antigone* ran from November 25 to December 10, 2000.

ABBREVIATIONS

The standard abbreviations of the titles of Sophocles's three Theban plays are:

Antigone:	Ant
Oedipus the Tyrant:	O.T.
Oedipus at Colonus:	O.C.

LINE NUMBERING

The line numbers accompanying the text refer to the English translation. The line numbers at the top of each page refer to the original Greek text.

DEDICATION

This translation is dedicated to the memory of

ROBERT FRANCIS KENNEDY

who loved Greek tragedy and, in the year of my
own birth, perished in his attempt to enact the
Classical ideal of public life.

In our sleep,
pain which cannot forget
falls drop by drop upon the heart
until, in our own despair,
against our will, comes wisdom
through the awful grace of God.

Aeschylus, *Agamemnon*, 176

ANTIGONE

Enter ANTIGONE *and* ISMENE

ANTIGONE

O my own dear sister, Ismene,
Do you know of a single evil, among all the sorrows of Oedipus,
Which Zeus has not yet fulfilled in our two lives, his daughters?
In our troubles I have seen nothing painless,
Nothing free of ruin, shame, dishonour;
And what is this announcement, that even now
The General declares to all the city's people?
Do you know? Have you heard of it? Or have they eluded you,
These evils coming from our enemies and toward our
                                                dear ones?

ISMENE

No story has come to me, Antigone, of dear ones: 10
Neither sweet nor painful, since we two were bereaved
Of both our brothers on a single day, each by the other's hand
Destroyed. But since the Argive army vanished in the
                                night, and now is gone,
I know of no events more recent, whether happy or disastrous.

ANTIGONE

I knew that well, and summoned you on that account
Beyond the courtyard, that you alone might hear me.

ISMENE

What is it? Your face is coloured by some secret.

ANTIGONE

Creon has exalted one of our brothers with burial.
He has withheld it from the other, and dishonoured him –
Has he not? They say that Eteocles is hidden in the ground,   20
With justice and just treatment under law, below, among
                                the honoured dead.
But the corpse of Polyneices, who died in agony,
All citizens are forbidden, by decree, to hide with burial
Nor may anyone lament him, but he goes unwept, unburied,

And far-sighted carrion birds are glad of their sweet treasure.
The good Creon, they say, has made announcement to you
And to me – I do include myself – of these affairs,
And now he comes here to proclaim to those who have not heard,
That it be clearly known: even to begin this deed, in the
                                                    least degree,
Whoever does so, his portion shall be public execution.   30
Thus stand your affairs; and you will soon show
Whether you were born with a noble nature,
Or as the wicked daughter of a noble line.

ISMENE
My sad-hearted sister, if circumstances lie thus,
What could I gain
By loosening or tightening their strings?

ANTIGONE
Think on it: will you work with me, and be my ally?

ISMENE
How great is the risk? What have you in mind?

ANTIGONE
Whether you will take up his body,
With this hand.   40

ISMENE
Do you really mean to bury him, though the city forbids it?

ANTIGONE
He was, whether you approve or not, your brother and mine.
I will never be condemned as a traitor to him.

ISMENE
O stubborn heart! Despite Creon's decree?

ANTIGONE
It is not for him to keep me from my own.

ISMENE
Oh, me! Consider, my dear sister, our father:
How he perished in infamy, despised;
Self-convicted for his double fault,
Working his own will he struck his eyes
With his own hand: when his wife and mother – one
                                                double word –   50
Destroyed her life in the twisted noose.
Thirdly, our two brothers on a single day ruined one another,

One miserable fate in common, accomplished by each
                                        other's hands.
Now consider us two survivors, how most horribly we
                                        would die,
If against the law's force we should transgress our
                                        sovereign's will;
But think on this, you must: we are by nature women
And it is not for us to do battle with men.
Therefore are we ruled by the stronger,
And must heed his decree; this, and worse yet.
For me then, I beseech this ground's genius   60
To hold out pardon: even if it injure me
I shall obey those who have come to power.
And to do too much is to be heedless.

ANTIGONE

No more will I ask you, and no more,
No matter if you yet should find yourself
Willing to perform it, shall you share in my sweet labour;[1]
But know: however it appears to you,
I will bury that man. To die for this
Seems to me noble: I shall lie down with mine own,
And my brother with me, having dared to be pious.   70
For I must please those down below for a longer time
Than I must please these here, since I shall lie there forever.
But you, dishonour what the Gods hold worthy of honour,
As you see fit.

ISMENE

I have done them no dishonour, but by nature
I have no guile to act against the power of the State.

ANTIGONE

You may well say so. But I shall find a way
To heap up burial upon my dearest sibling.

ISMENE

O wretched woman, how I fear for you —

ANTIGONE

Fear not for me, but set your own fate in order.   80

ISMENE

Disclose this deed to no one; keep it hidden
As our secret, as I shall with you.

ANTIGONE

    Oh, speak it out! If you keep silent,
    If you fail to make a public proclamation,
    You will be far more hateful to me.

ISMENE

    A hot heart you have, for cold affairs.

ANTIGONE

    But I am certain I delight those whom I must.

ISMENE

    If indeed you can: but you ask the impossible.

ANTIGONE

    Not so: I will stop when my strength fails.

ISMENE

    Unseemly, to begin a hopeless task.   90

ANTIGONE

    If those are your sentiments, I will hate you
    And justly will the dead despise you as their enemy.
    Therefore leave me to mine own poor counsel
    To suffer this extremity: but no penalty can befall
    So great as to deprive me of a noble death.

                   [Exit Antigone on the spectators' left

ISMENE

    Go then, if you see it thus. But know,
    You move on thoughtlessly,
    Though rightly dear to your dear ones.   *[Ismene retires into the*
                             palace by one of the two side-doors

               Enter the CHORUS

               First Choral Ode[2]

CHORUS

    Beam of the sun, most beautiful of lights
    That first shone on seven-gated Thebes,
    At last you are revealed   100
    Golden eyelid of the dawn
    Mounting on the Dircean streams.
    The white-shielded Argive all in armour was expelled,
    A fugitive running onward, driving with a sharper rein
    Who from our land because of Polyneices' quarrel,

Bitterly shrieking like an eagle flew above the earth,
Wings covered in white snow, carrying countless weapons
And helmets plumed with hair of horses;

And standing his murderous spearmen in a ring   110
That gaped around our seven-gated city,
He left before our blood could fill his jaws;
Before the pinewood torches of Hephaestus
Could take our crown of towers.
So far the crashing noise of Ares ran,
Raised loud around our backs;
A grievous wrestling of the dauntless serpent.
For Zeus despises the noise of a boasting tongue;
And seeing them coming like a mighty stream
With the arrogant din of clanging golden arms,   120
He cast at one His spear of fire
Who moved upon the highest citadel
Already hastening to cry, *Victory*!

Down upon the solid ground he fell,
Swinging, still carrying his fire
Who with the mad motions of the Bacchanal
Exhaled the blasting winds of his most hateful wrath.
But his threats miscarried;
And here and there gigantic Ares in the lead
Dealt out, upon the rest, His grievous blows.   130
For seven captains, ranged against their equals
Before our seven gates
Left behind the brazen tribute
To Zeus who turns the tide of war:
Except two miserable men
Born from one mother, one father;
Each was poised upon the other's spear
And took his portion of their common death.

But since the mighty name of Victory
Came to Thebes of the Chariots   140
Whose rejoicing answered hers,
After this late war let us forget
And turn to the nightlong Chorus

At all the temples of the Gods,
And let the Chorus leader be the Bacchus of Thebes
Who shakes the earth.
But this king of our land,
By the recent dispensation of the Gods,
Our leader new, Creon son of Menoeceus –
At what thought is he working   150
That he has called this gathered synod of the elders
Sending us all the summons?

Enter CREON

CREON[3]

O men, our state's affairs were shaken
With tremors many and severe; but the immortal Gods
Have safely set them right again. Therefore by messengers
Have I caused you out of all our folk to join me here,
Knowing that you well reverence the eternal power
Of Laius' mighty throne, and that when Oedipus ruled
And steered the city straight, and when he died,
You cared for all the issue of that house   160
With steadfast thoughts and loyal. Therefore,
Since on a single day those brothers were dispatched
By double portions of a single fate, striking and stricken
And stained with a kinsman's murder,
I now hold all the power and the throne
By kinship closest to the heirs who perished.
Now, one cannot know the thoughts and the mind
And the soul of a man, until he has been shown
Tested by the duties of his rule, and by his laws.
For any man who rules a city, and will not cleave   170
To the best of plans, but out of fear confines his tongue –
Such a one has always seemed to me to be the worst of men,
And so I still believe. And any man who owes allegiance
Greater to his own dear kin than to his country,
I call that man no man at all. For I –
And may Zeus know this, who watches all men always –
Should I see ruin coming on our town
In sweet salvation's stead, I would not be silent;
Nor would I ever call my own

A man who moved against this realm   180
That is our saviour. And I know this:
That only while this ship of state sails evenly and well
Can we make our private loves.
Such are the rules by which I hope to prosper Thebes.
And now I hold it well proclaimed, to all the town,
Concerning those two brothers both,
The children all of Oedipus derived:
Eteocles, who perished fighting for this city,
Distinguished to the last degree for valour with the spear,
Is to be hid with burial, and all the rites over the grave   190
Which follow to the underworld
The corpses of the noble dead.
But this man's blood relation –
I speak of Polyneices – who returned from exile,
Willing to burn the land with fire,
Downward from the topmost stone;
To burn the temples of his people's Gods,
Who would have tasted his countrymen's blood,
Leading the remainder into slavery –
Of him the proclamation has been made   200
To this our city, that none may bury or bewail him in the
                                                          least,
That he be left unburied, his flesh disfigured
For all to see, a prey to the vultures and the dogs.[4]
Such are my intentions, and never on my account
Shall the wicked be honoured before the just;
But whoever is well-disposed toward our state,
Living or dead, he shall be honoured by me.

CHORUS
That pleases you, Creon child of Menoeceus,
Regarding this city's friend and its enemy;
And it is possible for you to use the law   210
However you will, over the dead
As over us living men.

CREON
And now, be watchful over this decree.

CHORUS
Set a younger man to bear this task.

CREON

But there are guards already posted round the corpse.

CHORUS

Then what is this that you command besides?

CREON

That you give no quarter to transgressors.

CHORUS

None is so foolish that way, as to love dying.

CREON

Indeed, that is the payment for it. But many times
A man has perished from the hope of profit.   220

Enter the GUARD

GUARD

My lord, I will not say that I come short of breath,
Having sprung here on light, nimble feet:
For many times I stopped to think,
And circled in the road and turned myself around,
For my soul kept talking and telling me,
Wretched man! Why go on,
Toward a place of punishment?
Miserable one, are you tarrying again?
And if Creon should hear the news
From some other man, how wouldn't you suffer?   230
And turning that sort of thing over and over in my mind,
With slow and halting steps I made my way
And thus the short road was made very long.
But in the end I managed to arrive here,
To come to you; and if I can say little,
I will speak nonetheless. For I come
Having grasped on to the hope
That I will suffer no more than my fate.

CREON

And what is this of which you seem so frightened?

GUARD

I want to tell you first about myself: 240
I neither did this thing nor knew who did it,
And if I came to harm for it, that would not be just.

CREON

You point your answer well,
And circle round the matter.
But you seem to have some news to tell me.

GUARD

The terrors of it make me hesitate.

CREON

Will you speak, have done, and be gone!

GUARD

I will tell you then. Just now, the corpse –
Someone got away with throwing earth on it,
Having strewn the skin with dry dust,   250
And performed the needful rights owed to the dead.

CREON

What say you? What man would dare perform this?

GUARD

I know not: for there was neither stroke of hoe,
Nor heaping up of earth by spade,
And the ground was hard and dry, unbroken,
Nor furrowed by the wheels of any carriage,
But the worker left no trace, whoever he was.
And when the first watchman of the dawn
Showed us the trouble, we marvelled, all of us.
The corpse had no entombing mound, but lay   Covered from   260
sight by a fine dust,
As though the one who got away had meant
The bare prevention of a sacrilege.
There was no sign that beast or dog had come,
Or torn the corpse with teeth. And then
There was commotion as we railed at one another,
Guard accusing guard with evil words,
Until at last we would have come to blows,
Nor was any present to prevent it.
For each one seemed to be the culprit   270
To the rest, though no one clearly was,
And all claimed total ignorance.
We were ready to take red-hot iron in our hands,
To crawl through fire, and swear great oaths,
That by the Gods, we did not do this thing

Nor plan it. At last,
When there was nowhere left to search,
Someone spoke, who caused us all to bow our heads
For fear, down toward the ground.
His advice none could contest, nor imagine   280
How to prosper if we followed it.
He said the story of it must be told to you,
That nothing of the deed should be concealed.
And that plan won the day, and I by lot
Was damned enough to win this happy chore.
Unwillingly I come here, and certainly
Unwanted; for no one likes the messenger
Of evil news.

CHORUS

Sovereign, my thoughts have asked me,
If this deed might not have been the work of Gods?   290

CREON

Stop, before your talk entirely fills me up with rage,
And lest I find you foolish, elder though you are.
Unbearable suggestion, that things divine
Have taken thought for this cadaver!
Do They honour him with burial as a hero,
Who came to burn the lofty-columned temples
And the shrines, and the very land –
Who scattered laws like chaff!
Or do you see the Gods rewarding evil men?
Impossible. No, but some certain men   300
Since first I issued this decree, have borne it
While in secret, murmuring against me;
Tossing their heads against my yoke, nor justly
Bending down their necks in meet submission to me.
By such men were these guards – I know it well –
Induced to do all this, for wages.
For nothing takes such root in men as wicked, silver coin,
That brings whole cities down,
And drives men from their homes; this it is,
That trains and warps the organ of invention   310
Twisting sound men's hearts
And setting them to shameful practice.

Money taught humanity to stop at nothing,
And master every gross impiety.
The hired men who did this thing
In time shall pay their debt to justice.
And, as ever Zeus retains my reverence,
Know this well, which to you I swear:
If you fail to find and set before mine eyes
The very man that made this burial,   320
Death alone shall not suffice for you
Until you hang alive, and make
Disclosure of this insolence
So that — since you know whence profit comes,
You may keep on grasping for it, having learned
Not to love prosperity from every source.
Ill-gotten, shameful riches ruin more men,
You will realise, than they save.

GUARD

Will you grant me speech, or shall I turn and go?

CREON

Don't you understand how painfully you've spoken now?   330

GUARD

Does it sting you in the ears, or in the soul?

CREON

Why do you reckon where my trouble stings me?

GUARD

The culprit has upset your soul; but I,
Only your ears.

CREON

Oh, you were clearly born to drivel.

GUARD

At least I never did this deed.

CREON

You did it, and you threw away your soul
For silver.

GUARD

Oh, monstrous — that a man should have suspicions,
If he suspect but falsely!   340

CREON

Make epigrams of your opinion now.

But if you cannot make the culprits manifest,
It will come home to you, that guilty wages
Make men wretched.

GUARD

May he duly be discovered! Whether or not
The man is apprehended, luck will decide it;
But you will not see me coming here again.
Even now, saved beyond my hope and expectation,
I owe the Gods much gratitude.

[Exeunt Creon and Guard

Second Choral Ode

CHORUS

Marvels are many, and none more marvellous than humanity,   350
That on the Southwest winter wind
Crosses the grey sea,
Ringed by depths of the engulfing waves:
And Earth, the oldest of the Gods,
Inexhaustible and deathless, humanity wears away,
With year after year the going up and down
Of ploughs, behind the turning offspring of the horse.

The blithe race of the birds, mankind ensnares;
And captive leads the tribes of wild beasts,
And living natures of the deep marine Within his woven nets, 360
ingenious man:
The mountain-roving animal,
That dwells abroad the open land,
He overcomes with cleverness;
The long-maned horse he tames
Laying the yoke around his neck,
And the tireless mountain bull.

He has taught himself speech,
And thought, swift as the wind;
The casts of mind that govern towns;   370
Taught himself to shun the frosty air,
And dark-shadowed arrows of the rain.
Man finds a way, everywhere;
Never at a loss, in all that is to be:

Only from death can he devise no escape,
Though his inventions cure
Unfathomable plagues.

Man possesses arts
Subtle beyond all hope of reckoning.
Now to the evil, and now to the great, he slowly moves: 380
Honouring the laws of earth
And swearing by the Gods to cleave to justice,
He exalts his city;
But without a city is the wicked man,
Because he dares all.
Never may such a person share my hearth,
Nor match his thoughts with mine,
Who does such things.

                Enter ANTIGONE, *led by the* GUARD

I half suppose this a holy sign –
I know it – I cannot deny   390
This is the child, Antigone!
O wretched one,
And child of a wretched father, Oedipus,
What is it? Surely you have not been arrested,
Faithless to the royal laws,
Taken in recklessness?

GUARD

This is she, who did the work. We caught her
As she was burying him. But where is Creon?

                Enter CREON

CHORUS

He comes at our need, returning from the palace.

CREON

What is it? What stroke of fortune warrants my return?   400

GUARD

My lord, there is nothing mortal man should swear
To be impossible: for hindsight
Makes our expectations false!
I could have sworn that I would not come back
For a long time, lashed by the stormy threats you made;

But with a joy beyond my hopes, surpassing any other
                                         pleasure
In its greatness, I have returned —
In spite of oaths that I would come no more —
Leading this girl, who was arrested at devotions
Tending the burial. And not by lot   410
Did this befall me! It is my own good luck,[5]
And nothing else, this thing. And now my lord,
This is she, just as you demanded;
Take her for questioning and cross-examination:
But I am honest, free and acquitted of these evils.

CREON
How and where did you arrest this girl you lead?

GUARD
She was burying the man herself —
You know it all.

CREON
You understand, and rightly mean the things you say?

GUARD
I saw this woman burying the body you forbade.   420
Haven't I spoken plainly, and clear?

CREON
And when she was taken, how did you see her
In the action of it?

GUARD
It happened thus: returning to our post,
According with your dread injunctions
We swept off all the dust that hid the corpse,
And slick with damp the body lay well naked;
Then sat we down upon the highest hill,
Sheltered from the wind, lest the escaping reek
Should reach us, and man moved man   430
To wakeful vigilance, with harsh reproof
If any wearied of his labour. A long time passed,
And in the middle of the upper air,
The bright disk of the sun stood burning,
When suddenly a whirlwind took a plume of dust
From off the ground, and stained the sky,
Filling all the plain, tearing from the trees their leaves,

And swelling out great reaches of the wind.
We shut our eyes, and bore
The scourges of the holy storm.   440
At great length, when it ceased at last,
This child was spotted, and we heard her
Keening with a sharp, embittered cry
As of some bird, that sees the nest-bed
Empty of its young, and is bereaved.
Even so she cried out when she saw
The corpse was bare of dust, and moaned
In lamentation, calling evil curses, in her prayer,
Upon the men who had performed that deed.
And with her hands she took up straight   450
The thirsty dust, and raising high
A hammered jug of bronze, poured out
Upon the corpse a threefold cornet of libations.
And seeing her, we started in pursuit;
But when we quickly closed with her,
She was not terrified. We demanded
Of her past and present deeds, but she
Sought no protection in denials. And for me
This was both sweet and grievous:
For it was sweet to have escaped from evils,   460
And grievous to lead a dear one into them.[6]
But all such things mean less to me
Than does my own salvation.

CREON
  You, then: you who hang your head down
  To the ground, speak! Or do you deny
  That you have done these things?

ANTIGONE
  I affirm that I did, and I do not deny it.

CREON [to the Guard, then to Antigone]
  Betake yourself wherever you wish, free
  From this heavy load of guilt.

                                          [Exit Guard
                    But you,
  Tell me briefly and with no addition: 470
  Did you know the edict that forbade this?

ANTIGONE
I knew. How could I not?
It was a public edict.

CREON
And yet you dared to overstep the law?

ANTIGONE
Yes, for the proclaimer of that law was not Zeus,
Nor was it Justice, who dwells together
With the Gods below: such are They who have
Prescribed the laws for human beings.
As for the laws that you announced,
I did not think them so strong   480
As to be able to prevail against unwritten
And unfaltering commands of the Divine,
Since you are mortal. For not just now,
Nor only yesterday, but always and forever
Do these live, and no one knows the dawn
From whence they came. I would not think
Of bearing the displeasure of the Gods, to pay
The dear requital of Their laws, for fear
Of any man's design. That I shall one day die,
I well knew. And why ever not?   490
That would be so, even without your proclamations.
And if I should die before my time,
I call that a fine prize. For whoever lives
As I do, among so many evils, how would he not
Hold it a prize to die? And thus for me
It is no grievous thing, to take this measure
Of my destiny. But if a man died
Who was born from out my mother's womb,
And I left him unburied, I would grieve for that.
This grieves me not. But if I seem to you   500
To happen upon foolish deeds, perhaps
I owe the foolish verdict to a foolish judge.

CHORUS
The child shows herself as fierce as was her father,
And she knows not how to yield before misfortunes.

CREON
But understand this well: that hard and stubborn spirits

Often fall; and the most solid iron, tempered in the fire,
You shall see shivered into fragments and destroyed:
I also know, the little bridle brings the angry horse to heel:
And no man thinks great thoughts who is his neighbour's
slave.[7]

[*to the Chorus*] She knew then how to mock established laws,   510
Overstepping them with hubris; when she had done so,
Her second hubris was to smile at the first,
Exulting in transgression. Now if this achievement lie
Unpunished on her, I am no man; rather, call her man then.
Even if she is my sister's child – even if she were
More near to me by blood than every worshipper of Zeus
Before the altars of our home – she shall not avoid
The bitterest of her portion. And I denounce her sister
For collaboration in this burial. Summon her as well –
Just now, inside, I saw her raving and beside herself: 520
For oft they stand accused of treason, even when the crime
Remains undone, whose hearts contrive their malefactions
In the dark. [*turns to Antigone*]
But this, too, I detest: a captured criminal
Who seeks to glory in her evils.

ANTIGONE

And having captured me, what more do you require
Than my death?

CREON

Nothing. When I have that, I shall have all.

ANTIGONE

Then why do you delay? Of all your words
There is none that I find pleasing, nor shall be ever;   530
While to you, my thoughts are just as hateful.
And yet, how could I win a greater fame
Than to lay mine own dear brother in the grave?
[*indicating the Chorus*]
All these would admit my action pleased them,
If their mouths were not sealed shut with fear.
But the sovereign power, blessed in so much else,
Can say and do as it sees fit.

CREON

Of all these Cadmean people, only you see it so.

ANTIGONE

They see; but you have stopped their mouths.

CREON

And are you not ashamed, to reason it so differently?   540

ANTIGONE

No: for to be pious toward those who once shared
My mother's womb, is nothing shameful.

CREON

Did not such a brother perish on the other side?

ANTIGONE

Blood siblings, from one womb, by the same father.

CREON

How then can you give honours which that brother
Would call sacrilege?

ANTIGONE

That brother is a corpse; he will not witness it.

CREON

But he will, if you honour him as equal with the criminal.

ANTIGONE

It was not a slave, but a brother who died.

CREON

That brother ravaged this land, while the other died   550
Defending it.

ANTIGONE

And yet the Death-God yearns for what is due Him.

CREON

But the good and useful man ought not to be made equal
To the wicked.

ANTIGONE

Who knows, but that those below may find it lawful?

CREON

An enemy is never beloved, not even in death.

ANTIGONE

I was born to share my brothers' love, not their hatred.

CREON

You are going down now; if you must love,
Love the dead. But no woman shall rule me,
While I live.   560

Enter ISMENE

CHORUS
  Look: Ismene by the doorway weeps
  A sister's tears, and on her brow
  The blushing clouds and scratches red
  Run down and wet her lovely face,
  Disfigured with her shame.

CREON
  And you, who lurk within my home
  And like some venomous serpent, undetected
  Drink away the vigour of my blood:
  Two ruinous women, fomenting their rebellion
  At my throne;   570
  Come, tell me – do you also say you had a share
  In this burial, or do you swear that you know nothing?

ISMENE
  I have done the work, if only she agrees with me,
  And then will I share the punishment, and bear it.

ANTIGONE
  But Justice will not allow you that,
  Since you were unwilling then, and I will not share.

ISMENE
  But among your bleak misfortunes I am not ashamed
  To make myself your fellow in suffering.

ANTIGONE
  Hades and the dead below share knowledge
  Of the deed; but I do not love my loving sister   580
  For her words.

ISMENE
  O sister, do not dishonour me; do not prevent
  My dying with you and my honouring our dead.

ANTIGONE
  Do not die with me, nor touch those deeds
  Which you did not perform. My death is enough.

ISMENE
  And what life could be dear to me,
  When you have left me here?

ANTIGONE

Ask Creon. You are his concern.

ISMENE

Why do you torment me, when it cannot help you?

ANTIGONE

If I mock at you, I suffer as I do it.   590

ISMENE

And yet, how might I help you, even now?

ANTIGONE

Save yourself: I will not hinder your escape.

ISMENE

O my wretched one, shall I be utterly left out of your fate?

ANTIGONE

You chose to live; I chose to die.

ISMENE

But not without my arguments, my words – [8]

ANTIGONE

You seemed to think nobly to those on one side;
I to those on the other.

ISMENE

And yet our guilt is equal.

ANTIGONE

Take heart: you are alive, but I died long ago
That I might serve the dead.   600

CREON

Of these two children I declare
That this one has been foolish for a moment;
And that one, since the moment she was born.

ISMENE

Not so, my king. The mind that nature grows in us
Does not remain through our misfortunes: it leaves us.

CREON

It left *you*, at least, when you chose
To practise crime with criminals.

ISMENE

And what life of mine could be worth living
Alone, without her?

CREON

Speak of 'her' no more; she is already gone.   610

ISMENE

    Then you kill the bride of your own child?

CREON

    He may plough some other field.

ISMENE

    Not according to what this girl

    And that man have agreed upon.

CREON

    I hate an evil wife for my son.

ANTIGONE

    Dearest Haemon, how you are dishonoured

    By your father!

CREON

    You pain me, you and your 'marriage'.

CHORUS

    Would you bereave your own son

    Of his girl?   620

CREON

    Hades will stop this marriage for me.

CHORUS

    It has been decreed, then. She is to die.

CREON [*indicating Antigone, and then both girls*]

    Decreed: for you and for me. Waste no time,

    But bring her inside, my servants. Henceforth

    These must be women, and no more live at liberty.

    For even brave men flee, when they behold

    Already the gates of Hades closing on their life.

                                     [*Exeunt Antigone and Ismene*

Third Choral Ode

CHORUS

    Happy are they whose lives have had no taste of evil.

    But for those whose house is shaken by the God

    No agony is missing, but it creeps upon the family entire, Like 630

    a wave; as when the wild storm wind out of Thrace

    Courses through the darkness of the sea,

    Rolling from the deep black sand

    And beating with its gales

    The face of the opposing shore.

Of the house of Labdacus I see the ancient sufferings
Falling in upon the sorrows of the dead;
No generation can redeem its progeny,
But some God throws all the family down,
And there is no escape. That light which lately spread   640
Upon the last roots of the house of Oedipus
Is now cut off, in bloody dust of the infernal Gods,
Through reckless speeches, and hearts deranged.

O Zeus, what insolence of men
Could ever circumscribe Thy power?
Sleep, that overcomes all things, does not arrest You,
Nor do the months divine, but through all seasons
You remain the ageless sovereign of Olympus'
Flashing brilliance. For the coming days,
And for ages hence, and all the past,   650
This is the law: no vast enormity
Can stalk into a mortal's life without disaster.

Far-wandering Hope comes as a benefit to many men,
But many men it cheats with vain desires:
Nor does such a one suspect what creeps upon him,
Until in heat of flame he burns his foot.
For there is wisdom in the famous saying:
To that man whose mind the Gods lead into ruin,
The evil comes to seem the good.
Though for the briefest moment he works on, without disaster;   660

Enter HAEMON

But here is Haemon,
Last born of your children and their last survivor,
Does he not come grieving for Antigone,
Desperate at the wicked loss of his young bride,
That was to be his wife?

CREON

We shall soon know, more clear than prophecy could tell.
My child, have you come here furious against your father,
Having heard my final edict of her death,
Who would have been your bride?
Or are you my dear for all, whatever I may do?   670

HAEMON

Father, I am yours. Since you possess and tender to me
Counsels good and needful, I will follow them.
For to me, no marriage is more worth the winning
Than thy good guidance.

CREON

This is the way, my son, rightly to compose your heart;
To stand behind your father's counsels in all things.
This is what men pray for, to have obedient children
Growing in the house, who will ward off the enemy
And pay honour to the friend, just as the father does.
But whoever begets a useless child,   680
What do you say of him, but that he makes
Abundant toil for himself, and laughter for his foes?
Do not now, my son, nor ever, for the sake of woman
And her pleasures, cast off reason; be aware
That the embrace grows cold wherewith an evil wife
Partakes of bed and household. For what greater wound
Can ever come about, than a dear one who is wicked?
Cast her off with loathing, just as if she were
Your open enemy, and let the child find herself
Some husband in the underworld. In sight of all the city,   690
Out of all the rest I chose this girl alone in her rebellion;
Therefore I will not wrong the city and make myself a liar:
I will kill her. So let her call and call again to Zeus,
Who keeps the bonds of blood that kinsfolk share –
Since if I tolerate disorder in my relatives by birth,
Then I must let it thrive in all men else.
The good man is he whose justice shows
In the city as well as in his home.
Now a criminal who oversteps the law,
Or thinks to give commands to those who rule –   700
Such a one can gain no praise from me.
But whomever the city appoints must be obeyed,
In each detail, whether just or utterly opposed to justice.
And I take heart, that the man who thus obeys
Would rule well, since he is well willing to be ruled,
And, stationed at his post, to hold the spear in hand,
Remaining there, a right and proper soldier.

There is no evil worse than anarchy.
This it is, that causes states to perish,
Makes houses desolate,   710
Disperses spearmen, routing their alliance;
But obedience to command
Saves the bodies of the fortunate many.
Therefore such rules must be defended
As are handed down, and they must not be
Weaker than a woman, ever.
It would be better, if deposition come,
That my usurper be a man! Lest someone say
That women are my betters.

CHORUS

It seems to us you speak this speech with wisdom,   720
If our old age has left us fit to judge.

HAEMON

Father, the Gods bring to bloom in human beings
By far the greatest of all possessions, namely Mind.
I cannot find a fault in what you say;
And I hope never to achieve that power –
And yet it may befall another man to reason well.
It is my natural portion to be vigilant
In your behalf, to note what people say
Or do or how they place the blame of things.
For fear of thy dread aspect, common men   730
Keep back whatever speeches you would not enjoy;
But it is mine to hear such things, in darkness:
How the city mourns this very girl, lamenting her,
Of all its women, as the one who least deserves to die
So wretchedly for deeds so full of noble fame:
For she will not allow her brother, fallen in the war,
To be destroyed by dogs or birds that prey on carrion.
Is not such a girl worth honouring with gold?
Words like these are spreading through the quiet dark.
There can be no possession I would honour more   740
Than your good welfare, O my father.
For what could be a greater honour to a son,
Seeing his father thrive in greatness,
Than to contribute something to him of his own?

At this moment, do not bear within you
One single thought alone,
Holding your own speech to be true, and none beside.
For whoever counts himself the only man to reason,
Or to speak, imagining that other men do not have souls –
Such people soon are opened, and their hollowness exposed.   750
But even if a man be wise, it is no shame
For him to learn much more, and not be adamant.
See how those trees that yield before the winter's flood
Are saved, e'en to the twigs,
While those that strain in opposition die,
Uprooted utterly. Just so the mariner,
Who in his power will not yield the ropes at all,
Must sail the remnant of his voyage with the keel
High in the air, the ship undone.
But let your anger slacken, and give ground.   760
For if despite my youth I may show forth my counsel,
I believe it would be better far if men were born
By nature full of perfect knowledge;
But because that cannot be,
And nature does not tend that way,
It is noble to pay heed to those who reason well.

CHORUS

My lord, to learn from him is right and fitting,
If he speaks according to the moment;
As it befits you [Haemon] to learn from him [Creon]:
For both of you have spoken well.   770

CREON

Indeed! For all the fullness of our age,
Are we to be instructed by a man so young?

HAEMON

There is no injustice in this; if I am young,
Look to my deeds and not to my years.

CREON

And is this such a 'deed' of yours,
To pay honour to defiant rebels?

HAEMON

I would not even ask that others honour evil people.

CREON

But this girl, is she not infected with transgression?

HAEMON

The whole Theban people denies it.

CREON

And will the city tell me how I am to govern?   780

HAEMON

See, how you have spoken this:
Like a very young man indeed.

CREON

Need I rule this country to the satisfaction of myself,
Or of some other?

HAEMON

There is no city of a single man.

CREON

Of the man in power: the city is
Considered his, is it not?

HAEMON

By yourself, you might rule a vacant country very well.

CREON

This man, it appears, is the woman's ally.

HAEMON

If you are a woman, yes: for in fact I am protecting you.   790

CREON

O worthless wretch, to have at your father with epigrams!

HAEMON

It is not right for me to watch while you do wrong.

CREON

And I do wrong, when I pay the pious homage due my
power?

HAEMON

You are not pious, trampling the honour of the Gods.

CREON

O polluted character, that follows after woman.

HAEMON

You will not find me pursuing ugly deeds.

CREON

Yet all your talk, at least, is on behalf of her.

HAEMON

And of you, and of me, and of the Gods beneath.

CREON

Never, while she yet lives, shall you marry that girl.

HAEMON   800

Then when she dies, some man will also put off life and die.

CREON

Are you so bold with open threats of opposition?

HAEMON

Why call that a threat, to speak against a hollow policy?

CREON

You will lecture on that through your howling,
Since you yourself are empty of intelligence.

HAEMON

If you were not my father, I should tell you
That you do not reason well.

CREON

You are a woman's slave; do not prattle
For my favour.

HAEMON

You prefer to speak, being the speaking man,
But not to listen?   810

CREON

Is that true? But understand this well,
Which by Olympus I swear:
Having berated me with insult,
You will not rejoice. Attendants,
Lead in that thing of hatred, that at once
And in the eyes and presence of her groom
She may die.

HAEMON

Not beside me shall she be killed: do not imagine it;
Nor looking with your eyes shall you behold my face again;
Go on then, rage among your intimates,   820
Against those willing to endure you.

                                                    [Exit Haemon

CHORUS

My lord, the man has left, quickly and in anger;
For at his age, the wounded spirit suffers heavy pains.

CREON

    I shall do it: let his feeling run beyond the bounds
    Of human nature, he will never save this pair of girls
    From their allotted doom.

CHORUS

    Then you intend to kill them both?

CREON

    No, not that girl who has touched nothing;
    For you speak wisely.

CHORUS

    And by means of what affliction would you kill her?   830

CREON

    There is a trail, desolate of mortal footsteps,
    Leading to a sepulchre of stone;
    Within it, I shall hide the girl alive
    With just so much to eat as holiness requires,
    So the whole city shall escape pollution.[9]
    And there perhaps she will pray to Hades –
    The only God this girl respects –
    And He may grant that she not die;
    Or else she may discover what prodigious, wasted toil
    Is her devotion to the dead below.   840

Fourth Choral Ode

CHORUS

    O Love, Thou art unconquered in the battle;
    Love, who dive upon our fortunes;
    Who, from the soft cheeks of a young girl,
    Keep'st Thy watch upon the night,
    And wend Your ways over the sea,
    And through the savage places:
    None of the immortals can escape You,
    Nor any human creature of a day,[10]
    But whom You claim, is mad.[11]

    You drag the hearts of just men   850
    Off their course into disgrace;
    Then they are just no more:
    And You have stirred this feud

Among men whose shared blood makes them kin.
But Desire, manifest in the eyes of this betrothed bride,
Prevails over the mighty laws, and sits beside them, strong.
For the Goddess Aphrodite vaunts in triumph where there
                                        is no battle.

Watching all this I find myself
Already swerving from the same decree;[12]
I lack the strength to check this stream of tears,   860
When I behold Antigone approach
That nuptial bed where all are laid to rest.

Enter ANTIGONE

ANTIGONE

See me, citizens of our fatherland,
Travelling my final road,
And gazing for the last time on the sunlight
I will never see again:
But Hades, who brings all down to sleep
Leads me alive onto the banks of Acheron;
Who have no share in the bridal hymn,
And none has sung to me my wedding song,   870
But I shall wed the river of despair.

CHORUS

And yet, as you go down among the hidden dead,
You do have fame, and praise: yours are not
The withering assaults of some disease
Nor grim retaliation of the sword,
But you alone among humanity
Shall go alive and willing into Hades.

ANTIGONE

But I have heard of a foreign queen,[13]
A Phrygian, Tantalus' daughter, who died in utter misery
Clinging like ivy to the heights of the mountain Sipylus,   880
Overcome, and slowly turned to stone.
They say the snowstorms wear away at her;
With nothing spared by the streaming ice
She waters with abundant tears
The mountain's wretched brow.
The fate that lays me down is most like hers.

CHORUS

But she was a Goddess, born from Gods[14]
While we are mortals, born to perish.
And yet, how great a thing it is, after your death
To have it said of you, that like a God   890
You bore the godlike hardship of your lot
Both as you lived and in your dying.

ANTIGONE

Oh, I am laughed at! Why, by the Gods of our fathers,
Will you not wait until I go, but abuse me to my face?
O, city! O wealthy citizens! O springs of Dirce River
And groves of Thebes, city of radiant chariots!
You at least I claim as fellow witnesses –
By what laws I journey to the prison of my sepulchre,
How I go to my unprecedented burial
Unlamented by my friends! Oh, me!   900
Homeless, miserable wretch!
Neither with the living nor the dead do I belong;
I am not dead and I no longer live.

CHORUS

Striding out toward the limit of audacity
You fell against the pediment of Justice.
Oh, child! A heavy fall! And this struggle
Is the debt your father left you.

ANTIGONE

You have touched on the most bitter of my cares –
The thrice-repeated heartache of my father's fate,
And all our wretched destiny – the great Labdacidae![15]   910
Oh, disasters of the mother's bed:
Her coupling with her son my father
Joined him to her, and her fate was ruin.
From such persons I was born to bear my mind in grief
Toward whom I go, unmarried and accursed,
To dwell with them. O my poor brother,
Achieving your own marriage,
You died and you destroyed me
Who survived you.

CHORUS

Pious action does approach true piety;[16]   920

But power and the man who wields it
Cannot let transgression last in any form:
And your own nature,
That insists upon its own decisions,
Cost you life.

ANTIGONE

Unlamented, friendless and unmarried,
In mental agony I lead myself along
This road whereof the ending is prepared.
Henceforth in my misery I lack the right
To see the eye of heaven's sacred torch: 930
And among my people, no one groans in mourning
For this fate of mine that makes no tears.

CREON [to the Chorus]

Don't you understand that if those songs
And lamentations before death were any use,
No one would have done with them?
Lead her, quickly! Enclose her
Within the vaulted tomb, as I instructed you:
Send her inside alone and desolate,
Whether she desires to die,
Or live entombed beneath that roof.   940
For we are pious as regards this girl:
She will be denied upward escape.[17]

ANTIGONE

O grave! O bridal-song! O home dug deep below,
That will be vigilant forever!
I do convey myself toward mine own,
Most of whom Persephone has greeted
At the gates of death: and I go down,
The last and the most criminal by far,
Before my span of life is run.
And yet I raise in me the mighty hope as I go on, 950
That I may come into the presence of my father
And be dear to him; dear to you, my mother,
And dear to you, my brother. When you died[18]
I washed you with these hands; arranged your limbs
And poured libations on the grave.
And now, Polyneices, this is my reward

For laying out your body. And yet,
In the judgment of the wise,
I have well honoured you. Indeed,
If I were a mother of children, Or if I had a husband who had   960
died and lay decaying,
I never would have undertaken this ordeal
Against the power of the citizens.
What is the standard I obey, in speaking thus?
If a husband of mine died, there might come another;
And children from a further man,
If I were bereaved again:
But from my mother and my father
That in Hades lie concealed,
No brother, ever, can be born.   970
By such a law as this, dear visage of my sibling,
I have honoured you foremost, though by my deeds
I seem to Creon to have broken law,
And taken on and dared things terrible.
And now, arresting with his hands
He leads me thus, unwedded, with no song
Of bridal celebration, nor a share of married life
And no part in the getting of a child,
But thus bereft of all my dear ones
I go alive and damned into the hole   980
Of dead humanity. How could I evade
The justice of the Gods?
What need I still look to Them,
Whose lot is misery? To what ally can I cry?
When I have gained impiety's disgrace,
For all my piety! And if in the Gods' sight this is fair,
Then I shall understand my fault when I have suffered for it.
But if these men are in the wrong,
May they suffer no more evil
Than the injustice they do me.   990

CHORUS

These same stormwinds of the soul
Still hold this woman.

CREON

The slowest of these men that lead her

Will have tears to weep for it!

ANTIGONE

O, that word arrives the nearest
Toward my death.

CREON

I give you no encouragement to hope
That this will fail of its fulfilment.

ANTIGONE

O Father City of the Theban land,
And our ancestral Gods,   1000
No more am I waiting to be led away.
[*To the Chorus*] Behold, you that are the
                                        Lords of Thebes,
The last remaining royal daughter of the kingly line:
How I suffer at the hands of men like these,
A pious woman, keeping holiness.

                                        [*Exit Antigone*

Fifth Choral Ode[19]

CHORUS

Even the form and figure of Danaë
Suffered, to exchange the light of heaven
For the darkness of the brass-bound prison yard,
Hidden and restrained within the tomb-like inner chamber.
She too – O dear child – was of exalted birth,   1010
And she became the keeper of the seed of Zeus,
That streamed with gold. The power of Fate is terrible,
Whatever fate it is; and neither wealth nor war,
Nor fire, nor dark ships crying out at sea, escape it.

And Dryas' child, the Edonians' sharp-tempered king,[20]
For his hateful rages was interned by Dionysus
In a prisonhouse of stone. And there
The aweful bloom of his insanity was withered.[21]
When that man came against the God with mockery
And insolence, he came to know his madness.   1020
For he stopped the Bacchic women, who cry 'euoi!'
And swing fire in their divine possession,[22]
And he angered the flute-adoring Muses.

Near to the waters of the Kyeneai,
The waters of that double sea,
Lies the headland of the Bosporos,
And Salmydessus, the Thracian city[23]
Where the War-God, who lives nearby,
Beheld the cursed, blinding wound of Phineus' two sons,
Inflicted by his savage wife,[24]   1030
Which left the circles of their eyes
Bereaved of sight, and yearning for revenge,
Having been stricken by her bloody hands
And the point of her weaving-needle.

And they languished idle there,
Weeping in their useless state,
Born from a mother most unhappily married.
But she was of an ancient lineage,
And derived from Erechtheus;
In distant caves, among the storm-winds   1040
Of her father,[25] this daughter of Boreas
Was raised, swift as horses on the steep,
The child of the God. But the Fates,
That last long, held even her, O Child.

Enter TEIRESIAS, *led by a boy*

TEIRESIAS

Lords of Thebes, we have arrived by one shared road,
Both of us sighted because one can see:
For that is the way of walking that remains unto the blind.

CREON

What is it, O aged Teiresias, now?[26]

TEIRESIAS

I will teach. And you, obey the prophet.

CREON

In the past I have not strayed from your advice.   1050

TEIRESIAS

Then guide aright the ship of state.

CREON

I am by experience equipped
To bear sure witness to the benefits thereof.

TEIRESIAS

Take thought: you walk once more
Upon the razor's edge of Fortune.

CREON

What is it? How I shudder at your mouth!

TEIRESIAS

You shall know, when of my art you hear the signs.
For entering my ancient seat of augury,
A gathering place of all the birds,
I heard a loud, strange birdsong shrieking   1060
In a horrible frenzy, uttering gibberish.
And then I knew, that with their talons
They tore at one another in the throes of murder.
For the beating rush of wings meant more than nothing.
Full of fear I quickly set about the burning of an offering
Upon a fully kindled altar. But from the sacrifice
Hephaestus[27] did not glow. Instead, upon the embers
Fluid drizzled, and it smoked and sputtered upward,
And bile was burst out high into the air,
And the dripping thighbones were laid bare   1070
Of all the layered fat that had enclosed them.
I learned it from this boy, that this was how
My divination from the rites had come to nothing.
For he guides me, as I guide others.
And the city is afflicted thus
Because of your decisions. All the altars,
Great and small, the North Wind has defiled
With birds and dogs come from the corpse
Of Oedipus' miserable, fallen son.
Therefore the Gods accept no more   1080
Our sacrificial prayers, nor flames
From thighbones wrapped in fat;
Nor does any bird cry out in signs discernible,
Now they have fed upon a man's rich blood.
So think on these things, child.
For every human being does make deep mistakes:
But when a man has missed his mark,
He is not yet unmanned, nor yet undone
Though fallen into hardships,

Who heals himself, and is not idle. Yes,   1090
Stubbornness is rightly called stupidity.
Give over to the dead man's claim,
And do not stab one who has perished.
What strength is this, to kill a corpse again?
I speak soundly to you, in benevolence:
And it is sweetest to pay heed
To someone speaking well,
If he should speak to your advantage.

CREON

Agéd sir, you fire it all at *this* man, [*indicating himself*]²⁸
As archers do, who shoot into their target;   1100
Nor am I unmolested by your wizardry; for years
By men of *that* kind,²⁹ I have been bought and sold
Like cargo rendered to the buyer's ship.
Make a profit if you like;
Trade in electrum from Sardis
Or the gold of India.
But do not hide him in the grave:
Not even if the eagles of Zeus,
Wishing for a meal, and seizing on him
Should carry him to Zeus' throne –   1110
Not even then would I, in fear
Of this pollution, let that man
Be buried! For I well know
That no man can defile the gods.
But the very clever mortals fall,
Old Man Teiresias, their falls most shameful
When they speak ugly words in lovely guise
For profit's sake.

TEIRESIAS

Pheu.³⁰ Does any human being know –
Does any say –   1120

CREON

What? What epigram is this?

TEIRESIAS

That of all possessions, prudence
Is by far the strongest?

CREON

   By just so much, I think, the failure to be wise
   Is full of pain.

TEIRESIAS

   You brought about this plague
   Upon our altars.

CREON

   I have no wish to trade reproaches with a wizard.

TEIRESIAS

   And yet you do so, claiming that my prophecies are lies.

CREON

   Yes, for all the race of prophets is in love with silver.   1130

TEIRESIAS

   And the tribe of kings adores ill-gotten gains.

CREON

   Do you realise, as you utter your remarks,
   That what you say refers to one who rules?

TEIRESIAS

   I do! For through me you have become
   This city's saviour.

CREON

   You are a clever prophet, but you love injustice.

TEIRESIAS

   You provoke me to declare those secrets
   That were better hidden motionless within my heart.

CREON

   Move them. But speak only if there is no benefit at issue.[31]

TEIRESIAS

   Oh, as things stand, I think I shall describe your fortune
                                          that way.   1140

CREON

   Rest assured, you cannot speculate upon my mind and policy.

TEIRESIAS

   But understand this well: not many still remain to you,
   The racing courses of the sun you shall endure
   Before a man who comes from your own flesh
   Shall have exchanged his corpse in due requital
   For those lifeless bodies – [32]
   Since you have ruthlessly thrown down a living soul,

Compelling her to dwell within the grave,
And kept a dead man from his burial rites,
Unhallowed, with no offering to grace his tomb   1150
Though he belongs to the Divinities below.
You have no claim in such affairs, nor do the Gods above
To whom you offer violent offence.
Because of these dead, the Furies wait for you —
The punishing destroyers in the Death-God's service —
And they will take you, these same monstrous powers.
Consider whether bribery has made me say these things;
For before long, the screams of men and women in your home
Shall be manifest. And all the hostile cities are enraged,
Whose soldiers' scattered limbs are hallowed[33]   1160
By the beasts and dogs, or by some plunging bird
Carrying polluted flesh into the cities
Where those soldiers had their hearth fires.
With such a sort of arrows — true and heart-rending —
I have shot you through the mind — for you grieve! —
Whose burn and stinging you shall not outstrip.
[*to his boy*] Child, lead us home again,
That he may hurl his rage at younger men
And learn to keep his tongue more quiet,
And to bear a better mind within his breast   1170
Than he can carry now.
                              [*Exit Teiresias, led by his boy*]

CHORUS
My Lord, the man left uttering dread prophecies;
And I warrant you, in all the time since my dark hair grew
                                                            white
I never yet heard this man speak a false word in the city.
CREON
I have marked that well,
And it churns my heart with worry.
For it is terrible to yield,
But terrible to take the other side,
Resist, and blast a curse onto my head.
CHORUS
O Menoeceus' son, you must take thoughtful care!   1180

CREON

But what must I do? Tell me, I shall obey!

CHORUS

Go, and bring the girl up from that deep and hateful prison,
And perform a burial for him that lies exposed.

CREON

These are your wishes? Seems it right that I should yield?

CHORUS

With all haste, my Lord! For the Gods' swift punishments
Cut off the wicked-hearted.

CREON

O me! In tribulation then,
I give over my resolve, that I held dear;
For ruin is not rooted in Necessity.

CHORUS

Go and do this now, and turn to nothing else!   1190

CREON

With all the speed I have, I go! Attendants one and all,
Take up work tools in your hands
[*pointing*] And bring them to that place in view;
For my part, since my policy has turned thus,
Having bound her, I myself shall liberate her.
For I fear and do believe it: best
Is to preserve the ancient precepts of the Gods,
Throughout life, till the end.

[*Exit Creon*

Sixth Choral: Dance Song[34]

CHORUS

O Thou of many names,
Glory of the bride that Cadmus' daughter was,   Thou child of   1200
deep-thundering Zeus,
Thou protector of the far-famed Italy;
Deoûs art Thou in the Eleusinian Plain,
Ringed by mountains and welcoming all;
As *Bacchus* you dwell in Thebes,
Mother-city of the Bacchae,
Beside the wood where flows the river Ismenus,
Upon the field where dragon spores once lay.

How oft the blaze of smoking torches
Hath caught sight of Thee,   1210
Above the two peaks,
Where the Corycian nymphs run, Bacchanalian,
Hard by that Castalian stream.
From the slopes of the Nyssian hills,
Adorned in ivy,[35] green and golden,
And the shores and headlands, thick with grapes,
Are You summoned;
Thou overseest thy revels in the Theban streets,
While they cry '*euoi!*'[36] with immortal words.

You honour Thebes above all other cities,   1220
As thy mother does, who knew the thunderbolt.
And now again, as the entire town
Is held fast by a violent disease,
Come! over the hillsides of Parnassus
On thy purifying feet
Across the rushing strait!

You lead the fire-breathing stars in dance
And watch over their wild songs at night;
Child of Zeus' fathering, Lord,
Appear together with Your nymphs divine   1230
That each night rave and dance Your chorus,
O Iacchus, dispenser of fortunes.

Enter PAGE

PAGE
Cadmus' neighbours, dwellers within the walls
That Amphion his son erected,
No form of human life would I disdain or praise
As fixéd and enduring:
For chance sets right, and chance casts down,
Both thriving men and wretched ones, forever.
To mortals there is no prophet can divine
The measure of these fortunes.   1240
For Creon was full praiseworthy, to my mind,
Saving this Cadmean ground from enemies,
And taking up the helm of sovereign power absolute,

He steered it straight;
And he throve in the begetting
Of his well-born children.
And now he loses everything.
For when men make forfeit of their pleasures,
Oh, in such a man I find no life, but an ensouléd corpse.
If you would, grow wealthy in your home;　　　　　　　1250
Put on the tyrant in your living:
But if you lose the gladness of it,
I would not hold the rest worth more for man
Than the shadow of a wisp of smoke, compared with joy.

CHORUS

And what is this burden you come bearing,
Of news for the royal household?

PAGE

Death. And the living are responsible.

CHORUS

Who has murdered? And who lies dead? Tell!

PAGE

Haemon has perished:
Bloodied with the selfsame hand.[37]　　　　　　　　　1260

CHORUS

Was it his own hand or his father's?

PAGE

He slew himself, angry with his father
For the homicide.

CHORUS

O prophet, how utterly you vindicate your word!

PAGE

That much is so; and now
You must consider all the rest.

Enter EURYDICE

CHORUS

But wait! Methinks I see the grieving wife of Creon,
Eurydice, out from the house by chance,
Or having heard about her child.

EURYDICE

O my townsmen, all of you,　　　　　　　　　　　　1270

I have heard the words,
As I rushed into the road
That I might come praying to Pallas Athena,
And it chanced that as I loosed the bolt
Upon the doors to draw them back,
A dreadful cry of household misery
Was hurled into mine ears,
And down upon my back I fell,
In terror for my family, and fainted.
But come, and tell whatever story you have left: 1280
For I will hear it, as a woman well acquainted with disasters.

PAGE

Dear Mistress, I shall speak as one who witnessed it,
Nor leave unsaid a word of what is true.
For why should I make soft for you
What later would reveal me as a liar?
The truth is always right.
I went with your husband as a guide
Up to the lofty plain, where still
Polyneices' body lay, torn ruthlessly by dogs.
And for him, we begged of Pluto   1290
And the Goddess of the Roads[38]
To stem Their rages,
And washing all within a sacred bath,
Wherein we placed the fresh-cut branches,
We burnt all that remained,
And built a high-roofed tomb
Heaped up with his native earth;
And then we turned aside,
Toward the young girl's wedding-grave,
To enter on that sunken house of Hades,   With its granite   1300
bench.
But someone heard a voice cry out
From near the riteless, mourning bridal chamber
And he came and told the Master Creon.
And as the king drew near, about his ears
There burst the unmeaning noises of a wretched scream:
And wailing in his grief, he set his bitter word astir:
O miserable self! Am I a prophet? Do I now crawl the road

Most horrible of all my travelled roads?
My child's voice greets mine ear! But, my henchmen, 1310
Quickly, go closer, and when you stand before the tomb
Pass through the fissure where the building stones
Have been removed to make a mouth into the cell;
Look there, and see if I heard Haemon's cry,
Or if some God deceived mine ear.
We looked to these commands of our despondent Lord.
Then at the furthest station of the tomb
We saw her, hung by the neck in a noose of linen
Fastened to the roof. We saw him,
With his arms thrown round her waist, lying prone, 1320
Bewailing his poor girl's destruction,
And the father's actions, and the ruined bed of marriage.
And Creon, when he saw him, rushed in close
Loud with agony, and shouted to him, calling
O wretched man, what have you done?
What sort of mind have you?
Amid what circumstance are you destroyed?
Come out, child, I humbly beg you!
And the son cast about him with eyes wildly staring,
With his face madly folded, and without a word 1330
He drew his sword with the double hilt, and slashing out
He came just short of his retreating father.
Then the miserable one felt rage against himself
And as he held the sword, he stretched tight and drove it on,
The blade between his ribs, into his side to the half-depth.
While there still remained some mind in him,
He held his girl in feeble, sodden arms
And breathing sharp and hard, expelled bright drops of blood
In a stream onto her brilliant cheek. There he lies now,
A corpse beside a corpse, having finally attained 1340
His wretched wedding, in the chambers of the Death God,
Having shown for all mankind, that lack of wise advice
Is the worst of all evils.

[*Exit Eurydice*

CHORUS
What do you make of this: the lady is gone,
Without a word of joy or sorrow.

PAGE

    I marvel at it too; and cherish hopes
    That hearing of her child's pain
    She has not thought it right to grieve before the city
    But beneath her roof at home, she will set before her women
    This calamity for tears and groaning.   1350
    For she is versed in circumspection, and will not do wrong.

CHORUS

    I do not know: to me, the dark foreboding is no better
    When deep silence broods, than when vain shouts are made.

PAGE

    But I will go to her home, and learn inside
    Whether she hides within her furious heart
    Some secret resolution. For I think you spoke well:
    Where there is heavy silence, astonishment waits.

                                         [*Exit Page*

Enter CREON, *on the spectators' left, with attendants,
    carrying the shrouded body of Haemon on a bier*

CHORUS

    And now this same king comes,
    Bearing in his arms a token of remembrance,
    Having wrecked himself, if right divine should speak,[39]   1360
    Upon no other ruin but his own mistake.

CREON

    Oh, the hard bereavements, from my stupid will!
    O, you elders all, look upon my kinsfolk that have killed
                                         and died:
    O me! My empty notions!
    Ah, oh! My child! Dealt young
    Your portion, of an early death,
    Ai-Ai, Oh, no!
    You have died and are gone,
    From my wrong thought, and not from yours.

CHORUS

    And oh, how all too late you seem to recognise   1370
    Justice!

CREON

    Oh, but I have learned
    The vile, sorry lesson of it:
    And then holding some heavy weight
    The God struck down into my head,[40]
    And drove me onto wild trails, alas!
    Where joy was overturned and trampled!
    Oh fie, fie, upon the cursed works of mortals!

Enter MESSENGER *from the house*

MESSENGER

    Master, it seems you come with sorrows on your hands,
    About to grasp yet others, in your house: 1380
    Soon you will behold them.

CREON

    Of all these evils, what evil yet remains?

MESSENGER

    The queen, my Lord, is dead, of a recent blow,
    The true and despairing mother of this corpse.

CREON

    O hungry gates of Death, insatiable!
    Will you kill me piece by piece?
    You come sent to me,
    O thou bitter messenger of pain,
    Crying what speech? *Ai-ai*,
    I was a dead man, and you killed me[41]   1390
    Yet again. What say you, boy,
    What new word for me now, Oh!
    Of my wife's bloody slaughter and undoing?

CHORUS

    You can see: for it is hid no longer.

CREON

    Ah, me! I see a second grief, another curséd loss.
    What Fate is waiting for me?
    In my hands I hold my child, bereaved,
    And I see before me one more corpse.
    Woe, woe, thou sorry mother, and woe, child!

MESSENGER

This woman let her eyelids yield to darkness,   1400
Dying by the altar on the sharp–edged sword
Having cried for the fate of Megarius, far-famed,
Who perished in the former days,
And then for this one [*indicating Haemon*];
And lastly she called down terrors
Upon thyself, the slayer of her children.

CREON

Ai-ai, Ai-ai, my fear has spread its wings.
Is there no one now, to drive the double blade into my breast?
I am reduced to misery,
Oh! Confounded with the dross of wretched misery!   1410

MESSENGER

She called you guilty of his sombre fortunes,
And of his.[42]

CREON

And by what sort of violence did she leave this life?

MESSENGER

When she learned of what her son had suffered
She stabbed her liver, and she screamed a sharp cry.

CREON

Oh me, my life! The blame of it can never move
And be affixed to some man's guilt, away from mine!
It was I, I, a useless man! who murdered you!
And I speak the truth! My servants, come!
And lead me off, as fast as you can go;   1420
Lead me as you would a man
Who is no more than nothing.

CHORUS

Your advice is for the best, if best there be
In so much evil. For greatest brevity is greatest strength
When troubles heap our feet.

CREON

Let it come, let the best of all fates come,
Let it appear, and lead me to my final day!
Come, and spare me looking on tomorrow!

CHORUS

    Those events will come; but what must now be done
    Amid what lies before you? For what will be   1430
    Is their concern, who must tend such things.

CREON

    But in that prayer I speak out all my wishes.

CHORUS

    Pray no prayers now! For there is no escape
    For mortals, from their fated circumstances.

CREON

    Oh lead me out, O child, a man of vanities,
    A fool, who killed you without willing it,
    And I killed you! this woman, my wife!
    O useless man! I know not where to turn;
    All in my hands lies utterly askew,
    And an unbearable Fate   Has driven down into my power. 1440
                             [*Exit Creon*

CHORUS

    Wisdom is by far the greatest part of happiness:
    Never dishonour what concerns the Gods:
    The grand words of the proud are paid with heavy blows
    That in old age have taught wisdom.

OEDIPUS THE TYRANT

The title of the play

Although Sophocles' play *Oedipus* is often called *Oedipus The King* or Latin *Oedipus Rex*, I chose *Oedipus the Tyrant* because that title better matches the sound of the traditional (though post-Sophoclean) Greek title *Oidipous Turannos*, and because I wanted to suggest the obstinacy and wilfulness Oedipus shows in his confrontations with Creon and Teiresias. Finally, part of what the Greek *turannos* denotes is the *irregularity* of the ruler's acquisition of power; that he comes to the throne either by force, or from a foreign country, or perhaps both. It seems to me that this word in Sophocles' title is bitterly ironic, because though Oedipus truly is the heir to the Theban throne, no one knew this when he became king – least of all himself. *Turannos* is not used of hereditary sovereignty acquired in the normal succession, the kind to which Oedipus was unwittingly entitled. To call him *turannos*, as Sophocles does in the course of the play, is to specify that he came to the Theban throne from *outside* Thebes (by answering the riddle of the Sphinx), and not by the hereditary succession which he nevertheless fulfilled.

Enter OEDIPUS, PRIEST *and* CHORUS

OEDIPUS

Children of ancient Cadmus, descended of him now,
Why do you come before me so, desperate in supplication
With wool and laurel garlands out of season?
The city teems with incense, and prayers,
And moaning. Nor do I hear these second hand,
From some messenger – I myself have come,
Children, to hear these things aright,
Whom all men call the famous Oedipus.
Therefore tell, O Elder, as befits your place,

On their behalf, what mood it is you stand in,   10
Yearning, or afraid? – So eager am I
All things to repair – for hard of heart
I should be, if your kneeling did not move me.

PRIEST

Great Oedipus who make me strong,
You see the diverse ages seated close
Before your altars; these who yet lack
The strength for far flight, and these
Heavy with age. I am a priest of Zeus,
And here are chosen boys yet unwedded –
And another crowd with wreaths sits   20
In the marketplace, before the two temples
Of Pallas Athena, where Ismenus
Plies his prophecies with ashes.
For the city, as you yourself perceive,
Already pitches and heaves its head from the depths,
And cannot stop the murderous rocking.
The land wanes, with fruit in calyx all unripe;
The herds are barren, the women childless;
And the fire-bearing God
With hateful plague drives diving through the city   30
By whom the house of Cadmus is made empty,
While dark hell grows wealthy with groans and weeping.
For these children and I sit at the hearth
Judging you to be, not like the Gods, but
First among men – in common affairs
As in demonic ones: and it was you
Who came to Cadmus' town and freed us
From the bitter tribute the relentless Sphinx demanded.
Alone you did it, and knew no more than we,
Untutored, unprepared – and as is known and said   40
You fixed it, and repaired our life.
And now, Oedipus mightiest in all men's sight,
We all beseech you in earnest, simple prayer:
Find us some strength. Hearing the voice of some God,
Or knowing from a man some source, speak,
Since tested people give the best advice.
Come, O noblest of mortals, and make the city straight.

Come, preserve your fame, for now this country
Lauds its saviour for his former zeal,
And may we never your great reign remember   50
Standing straight and later falling down!
But justify in steadfastness this city.
For then in augured birds you brought good omens
To us, and we are but the same nation now –
So if you will rule this land, as rule you shall,
Better reign over living men than empty ground,
Without a ship, a house, a tower, but desolate
And vain.

OEDIPUS

O piteous children, I know full well
Your yearning: I know you suffer, being ill –   60
And none among you therefore suffers so much
As myself: for the pain of all comes into one,
Alone, unto himself, and none beside.
My soul groans for the city, and for myself,
And for you, so that I rise sleepless –
And be aware, I have wept much, and many
A wandering road of thought have I gone down.
So searching have I found but this recourse,
And done it: I've sent Creon, Menoeceus' child,
Into the Pythia, at Apollo's shrine   70
That he might learn how, by action or command,
I may save this city. And already, counting the days,
I worry: what keeps him? For he is gone beyond
The term of such a journey – but when he comes,
I should be vile if I performed
One jot less than what the God reveals.

PRIEST

But you've spoken with luck – those penitents
Are waving to me now, that Creon approaches.

OEDIPUS

O Lord Apollo, may he come brilliant in fortune
With a bright face to bring salvation.   80

PRIEST

To guess from here, it bodes well – his head
Goes crowned with wreaths of berried laurel.

Enter CREON

OEDIPUS

    We will soon know; the distance draws,

    And we can hear him. O prince,

    My cousin son of Menoeceus, carrying what word

    Have you come from the God to speak to us?

CREON

    Good word. And if our woes are straightly overborne,

    They all will settle to the good.

OEDIPUS

    But what was the oracle? What sort of words?

    For what you've spoken gives me neither peace nor fear.   90

CREON

    If you require that these should listen too,

    I am ready to report it; or if you will, to speak inside.

OEDIPUS

    Speak before everyone. For the misery I carry

    Is for them, more than for my soul.

CREON

    Then may I say the words I heard from the God.

    Manifestly, the Lord Apollo rages at us

    Over a pollution of the country, which we harbour

    In this land. He rages, that we drive it out,

    And no more nurture this abomination

    Lest it grow incurable.   100

OEDIPUS

    And what cleansing? What sort of pollution?

CREON

    Banishment, or else new death requite old murder;

    For this blood overcomes our city in thunder.

OEDIPUS

    What kind of man does he denounce?

CREON

    There was among us, great king, a certain Laius

    Ruling before you came to steer the city straight.

OEDIPUS

    I am told that. I never saw the man.

CREON

    He died. And now the God demands, clearly,

The punishment by force of Laius' killers,
Whosoever they were.   110

CREON

But where in the earth are they? Where will the faded trace
Of this old guilt be found?

CREON

In this very land, according to the oracle –
And they can be found, it said,
Provided we take care lest they escape.

OEDIPUS

And Laius, is he murdered at home,
Or in a field, or in some other country?

CREON

He told us he was going to consult the oracle.
And being abroad, he was coming back home:
But he never arrived.   120

OEDIPUS

And no herald, no other pilgrim saw it,
Whose testimony one could use?

CREON

They all died – except for one, who fled in fear;
And he could only say one thing he saw for certain.

OEDIPUS

What sort of thing? For with one clue
We could discover many, and out of slow beginnings,
Take hope.

CREON

He said that thieves came on them, and killed the man
Not with one, but many men's hands together.

OEDIPUS

And how would any thief come into such courage,   130
Unless money was involved? A plot –

CREON

So it appeared. But Laius having perished,
The right man could not be found in the darkness that came on.

OEDIPUS

But what sort of darkness would prevent
A full inquiry in the murder of your very sovereign?

CREON

The riddles of the Sphinx compelled us, and her violence
Drove that other mystery from our attention.

OEDIPUS

But I will go back again, again show everything
From the beginning. Worthily has Lord Apollo,
And worthily have you, brought this case around   140
On the slaughtered man's behalf; so that with justice
Shall you see me allied, avenging God and Thebes together.
Not for some far-off friends, but for myself
Will I scatter this pollution from us. For whoever
Killed that king might soon attack ourself.
And so taking that king's cause, we help our own.
But rise, children of Cadmus, from these steps,
Praying with your wreaths of twisted wool and laurel,
And some attendant summon up the whole people,
Advised that I will try everything.   150
For we will be seen – or waxing with the God,
Or shining in our ruin.

PRIEST

Arise, my children, for this man has spoken out
The very grace for which we came here.
And may Saviour Apollo, sending this oracle,
Arrive and arrest our disease.

[Exeunt Oedipus, Priest, Creon

First Choral Ode

CHORUS

O sovereign speech of Zeus,
How do you incline to Thebes from golden Pythia?[43]
I am drawn upon the rack;
Fear and exhausting worry thrash my heart;   160
O Delian healer, called by our wild cries,
The sacred dread of You rises about me;
Either utterly anew, or else from long ago returning,
You compel old debts down the encircling years.
Speak to me, O voice immortal, child of golden Hope.

Daughter of Zeus, deathless Athena, first do I call upon you

And Your sister, protector of the land
Who sits enthroned within the marketplace's circle,
And Phoebus Apollo, who strikes from far away, oh
Shine on me Your threefold care to ward off death.   170
If ever before now ruin drove upon the city,
And You expelled the burning plague, come now!

Alas. Measureless sorrows I carry.
The whole people sickens,
And can find no sword of thought for its defence.
Earth bears no fruit; no birth relieves the women's keening
                                                        labour.[44]
One after another may you see them gone, like birds,
Swifter than wild flames, into the western shore of the
                                                    Death-God;

Of whose unnumbered loss the city perishes,
And at her feet her wretched children unlamented lie,   180
Carriers of death. Upon the altar-steps,
Young wives and mothers gray
Bewail in prayer the grievous chore before them.
So sighing as one voice, their paean shines;
For whose sakes, O golden daughter of Zeus,
Send clear-eyed strength.

Grant that Ares the destroyer, who burns me now,
Attacking without shield amid the screaming crowd,
May turn His back and run His course, far from our country,
Into the vast Atlantic, or the harbourless Thracian waves.   190
Whatsoever Night spares, Day seizes to destroy.
O Zeus, Father, dealing fire and lightning,
With thunderbolts stop Him.

Bright Lord Apollo, I pray Your rigid arrows
Scattered from the twisted bowstring may defend us;
And the lights of Artemis, flashing through the Lycean hills;
I call upon the gold-belted God, that shares His
                                          name with Thebes,
Bacchus dark with wine, companion of the Maenads
Among brilliant torches crying to Him 'euoi!'[45]
Approach us as our ally,   200

Against the God unhonoured among Gods.

Enter OEDIPUS

OEDIPUS

You pray. And what you pray for – if you are willing to receive,
And hearing my words to tend your illness,
You might take courage and relief from sorrows.
I will speak out about these things, foreign as I am
To the story of it and to the deed itself,
For I could not track it far alone
Unless I held some clue; but as it is,
Given that I was reckoned a Theban among Thebans
Only after these things took place,   210
I'll tell you all, Cadmus' children, these things:
Whoever of you knows the man by whom
Laius son of Labdacus was killed,
I command him to relate it all to me;
And if he fears for himself, let him remove
The retribution lurking in his way,
By himself, himself accusing.
For nothing more unpleasant shall he suffer
Than to leave the land, unharmed.
Or if someone knows a foreigner with guilty hands,   220
Let him not keep silent. For I will pay
Reward, and my thanks shall he lay in store.
But if you keep your silence, and fearing for some friend
Put from you my word and my requiring,
What I shall do then, you must hear from me now:
I do forbid that man – whosoever he is,
To be received by any person of this land,
Of which I am the sovereign and enthroned king;
To be spoken to with voice, pray in temples,
Sacrifice in company with us, or pass   230
The water-vessel at the rites.
From every house I banish him, as he is our scourge;
So has the Pythian seer of Apollo told us at the first.
Therefore I am the ally of the God, and of the slain man too.
I curse in prayer the one that did this,
Whether he hides alone or with some several men,

To smother out unhallowed his evil life in wretchedness.
I do condemn myself – if ever in my house
I knowingly make him my guest –
To suffer all the sentence I have just decreed.   240
I charge you to fulfil these things,
For me and for the God, and for this land
Forsaken by the Gods and fruitless in destruction.
For even if the God did not thus drive the case upon us,
We should be base not to investigate
When such a man, high-born and a king,
Is murdered thus. And now I do confirm it,
Since I have and keep the rule he held before me;
I have his bed, I have the wife who shared his seed.
And common children would we have, if that man had
                                           sired any –   250
If he weren't so unlucky getting heirs. But as it is,
Fate drove down into his power.
Therefore just as if he were my father
I shall fight for him, and through every trial
Searching shall I come, to take his killer down;
For Laius son of Labdacus, Polydorus' child,
And he the son of Cadmus, begotten by Agenor.
I pray that those who fail to do these things
Be ruined by the Gods – no harvest in the field,
No children from the women; but let them,   260
By their new condition, or a worse one yet,
Be thus destroyed. But you others of Cadmus,
Who see these things through, may justice fight for you
Always, and always the Gods be graciously with you.

CHORUS

As you have bound me to speak with this curse,
Lord, so shall I speak. For neither have I killed,
Nor can I show the killer. But as for whom we seek,
It was for sign-sending Apollo to declare
Whosoever it was that did the work.

OEDIPUS

Well said. But for a man to compel the Gods   270
When They're unwilling, is impossible.

CHORUS

I might say a second way, that appears to me beside these.

OEDIPUS

Even if there is a third, speak it out unsparing.

CHORUS

I know the Lord Teiresias can see as the very God sees;

And asking of him, my lord, one might most clearly learn

these things.

OEDIPUS

Nor have I left that out of my concern,

For since Creon spoke, I've twice sent messengers to

bring him –

And I marvel that he is not here.

CHORUS

Yet . . . aside from him, there was an old and blunted rumour . . .

OEDIPUS

Of what kind? I must examine everything. 280

CHORUS

He was said to have been killed by travellers.

OEDIPUS

I heard that too, but no one has seen the witness.

CHORUS

No, but if he has his share in human fear

He will not slight such dread commands as yours.

OEDIPUS

But if he fears no action, he will not fear words.

CHORUS

Yet there is one who will convict him.

For these already lead the godlike seer

In whom alone the truth of mankind inward blooms.

Enter TEIRESIAS, *led by a boy*

OEDIPUS

O Teiresias who know all things,

Teachable and unspeakable, of heaven and of earth, 290

Though you cannot see, you yet know in your mind

In what disease the city stands. And you alone,

Great Lord, have we found to be our saviour

And defence against the plague. For Phoebus,

If you have not heard it from the messengers,
Sent back the man we sent, answering
That freedom from this plague would only come
If, finding out who Laius' killers were,
We killed them, or drove them from the country.
Therefore, do not withhold what augury you know   300
From birdsong, nor any other path of prophecy within your ken;
The city and myself take into your concern;
Deliver all from death's pollution. We are in your hands;
A man's most noble labour is to give his aid,
From all the powers he has.

TEIRESIAS

Damn . . . damn . . . how terrible it is to understand
Where understanding is useless.[46]
I knew that well once, and I forgot it –
Or I would not have come here.

OEDIPUS

What is it? You've come so fainthearted –   310

TEIRESIAS

Let me go home. Most easily shall you bear
Your burden to the end, and I mine, if you consent.

OEDIPUS

You speak against all custom and all love for this your city,
Which turns toward you, while you hoard your wisdom.

TEIRESIAS

I see you speak at the wrong time;
And I will keep my silence,
Lest my suffering be like your own.

OEDIPUS

Do not refuse to speak if you have knowledge,
When, by the Gods, all we suppliants come beseeching you!

TEIRESIAS

All of you misunderstand. But let me never speak out   320
My miseries – lest I call them yours.

OEDIPUS

What are you saying? Though you know, you will not tell,
But think to betray us and destroy the city?

TEIRESIAS

I will not trouble you, nor myself.

What else will you accuse me of?
For you will not persuade me.

OEDIPUS

O you worst of evils, you would infuriate a stone!
Will you never speak out, but only stand, relentless?

TEIRESIAS

You deride my spirit: but you know not
What dwells inside your own. And you blame me.   330

OEDIPUS

And who would not be angry, hearing these words
By which even now you disregard the city?

TEIRESIAS

Even if I hide the words, the things will come.

OEDIPUS

If they must come, you must tell me of them.

TEIRESIAS

I cannot say more. Rage at it if you wish,
To the most savage fury of your heart.

OEDIPUS

My wrath is such that I will leave unsaid
Nothing of what I understand: therefore know,
It seems to me you conspired for this deed,
And so far performed it, all but killing with your hands.   340
If you could see, I should call the work yours alone.

TEIRESIAS

In truth? I tell you by that self command
You bid us all obey: from this moment
Never speak to these nor to myself:
For of this land thou art the wretched scourge.

OEDIPUS

So shamelessly you throw such talk at me?
Pray, how do you expect to escape?

TEIRESIAS

I am free, for the truth is my strength.

OEDIPUS

Where were you taught that? Not from your art.

TEIRESIAS

From you: for you made me speak, against my will.   350

OEDIPUS

What speech? Say it again, that I may learn it straight.

TEIRESIAS

You did not understand it then? Or are you baiting me to speak?

OEDIPUS

Not to retell what is known, but to say more —

TEIRESIAS

I say that you are the murderer, and the man whom ye seek.

OEDIPUS

But not unpunished shall you twice speak slander!

TEIRESIAS

Shall I unfold to you more yet,

That you may grow more angry?

OEDIPUS

So much as you can use —

Since you will speak in vain.

TEIRESIAS

It has eluded you, that with your dearest one   360

You are conjoined in the greatest shame

And do not see the evil of it.

OEDIPUS

You expect to blithely say such things forever?

TEIRESIAS

If there is some power in the truth.

OEDIPUS

But there is — though not for you: to you the truth is nothing,

Since you are blind, in your ears, in your mind, and in your eyes.

TEIRESIAS

Poor fool, to cast the very curses in my teeth

That soon every Theban soul will hurl at you.

OEDIPUS

Your life is one great night; and me,

And anyone who can see sunshine, you cannot harm.   370

TEIRESIAS

Your fate is not to fall at *my* hands —

Apollo is enough;[47] the vengeance of it all

Is His affair.

OEDIPUS

Is this Creon's invention, or your own?

TEIRESIAS

Creon is not your enemy, but you yourself.

OEDIPUS

O wealth, and power, and skill surpassing skill
In ceaseless competition, how great the jealousy
You summon in your train – if for this crown,
The gift the city gave me all unasked-for,
Placing it in trust within my hands – for this   380
The faithful Creon, dear from the beginning,
Should lust in undermining darkness to depose me
In secret league with a conniving, magical fraud –
A charlatan, whose eyes are keen to profit,
Blind to prophecy. Or if not, come, explain
Wherein you are this great divining genius.
How is it, that when that murderous riddling dog was here,
You said nothing that could liberate this town?
That enigma was not for some bystander to resolve;
No, a wizard was required. You were exposed   390
As having nothing known from birds, or from the Gods;
But when I came, the ignorant Oedipus, I stopped her:
I hit the mark by my own mind,[48] not learning from birds.
I whom indeed you struggle to unseat, expecting to attend
Hard by Creon's throne. I think you and your accomplice
Shall lament this scheme of driving out the scapegoat.
I think if you were not so old,
That you might learn from pain the final merit of your thoughts.

CHORUS

It seems to us his words were said in anger like your own,
O Oedipus, a mood that cannot help;   400
And that we may best unfold the portent of the God,
Let us look to it.

TEIRESIAS

King that you are, each of us is free to speak in turn;
That power, even I possess.
For I do not live as your slave, but Apollo's.
I need not Creon for my patron, but in mine own defence
Declare, that you have reviled me, that I am blind.
You are sighted, yet you do not see
That you are wretched; nor where you dwell,

Nor with whom you live;   410
Do you know from whom you come?
Nor do you know that of your parents,
Living and dead, you are the ruin.
One day in lame but terrible speed
The double whip of their compounded curse –
Mother and father, shall drive you from this country:
Now you see aright, but then . . . darkness.
What safe haven will not know your cries,
What reaches of the mainland shall be spared their speeding
                                                    echo,
When at last you come to understand   420
The wedding on which you embarked with such a fair wind,
Though your home is no harbour.
But a crowd of other griefs you cannot guess
Will make you the peer of your own children;
So drag the name of Creon, and my message, through the mud:
For never mortal man shall be so wretchedly destroyed as thou.

OEDIPUS
Can it be borne, to hear these things from him?
Go to ruin! Go, quickly! Get away from this house,
And never come back.

TEIRESIAS
I would never have come, had you not called.   430

OEDIPUS
I did not know what nonsense you would say,
Or I would not soon have called.

TEIRESIAS [turning and walking off]
That is what I am, as it seems to you –
An idiot; but to those who made you, I am wise.

OEDIPUS
What sort of – wait! –
Who among mortals made me?

TEIRESIAS
This very day will make and then dissolve you.

OEDIPUS
Everything you utter is so dark a riddle.

TEIRESIAS
But weren't you born the best at solving them?

OEDIPUS

 Mock me for that wherein you'll find me great. 440

TEIRESIAS

 Of course that very talent has destroyed you.

OEDIPUS

 If I have rescued Thebes, that does not vex me.

TEIRESIAS

 I am leaving now.
 [*to his boy:*] And you, lead me, my child.

OEDIPUS

 Yes, take him off; being where his presence grates,
 Make haste, that he never rankle me again.

TEIRESIAS

 I leave explaining why I came, not in fear
 Of your face. For by no means could you kill me.
 I say to you: this man, the one you searched for to arrest,
 Proclaiming your manhunt for the slayer of Laius — 450
 That man is here; a guest, a resident foreigner
 By reputation, who soon shall be revealed
 A true-born Theban, though he did not expect that happy hour,
 For from his vision, blindness; and beyond his wealth
 Homeless shall he trail his exile, feeling with a stick
 His way along the foreign ground. He shall be shown,
 That of those children of his house he is the brother
 And the father, and of her who bore him,
 He is the husband and the son;
 And of his father both the rival and the murderer. 460
 Go into these affairs, and reckon them:
 If you find I am mistaken,
 Say that I have no mind for prophecy.

    [*Exeunt Teiresias and Oedipus in different directions*

Second Choral Ode

CHORUS

 Who is it whom the oracle accused
 Of deeds unspeakable in bloody hands?
 The hour is come for him to drive his steps
 Faster than horses riding like a storm:
 For the Son of Zeus

With armament of fire and lightning
Leaps upon him;   470
And unfaltering
The dreadful Furies follow.

For the holy edict
Shines from Parnassus' slopes of snow,
And all things hunt the hidden man.
Bereaved, he ranges mad amid the wild caves,
And up the forest among stones
He wends his miserable footsteps
Like a bull,
Yearning to avoid   480
The prophecy that dogs him
From the centre of the world.
But his sentence is alive,
And it hovers on him, endless.

Withal how gravely hath the wise interpreter of birdsong
                                          moved me;
Whose word I cannot doubt nor yet believe; so shall I say it:
I am at a loss.
I fly at hopes, but cannot see the future, nor today.
For what quarrel there was made
Between the house of Labdacus, and Polybus' son,   490
In the past or present, I do not know;
I know of no feud that might be used
As evidence to move against the mighty reputation of our king,
And so avenge the house of Labdacus for its mysterious fall.

Zeus and Apollo know the lives of mortals utterly;
But though a prophet may discern more than I myself,
Yet there is no certain reckoning of truth;
Even if some man's wisdom overtake another's.
But may I never, till I see the word is straight, agree
When blame is cast.   500
Everyone knows: the man was seen to be wise
When the winged, girl-faced lion came against him,
And he stood our city in good stead –
Therefore in my heart I cannot call him criminal.

Enter CREON, *having changed from his*
travel-clothes into princely ones

CREON

Gentlemen citizens, having heard by rumoured, dire speeches
That King Oedipus denounces me, I have come, impatient.
If he believes that in our present crisis
He has suffered from my bringing him to injury
By word or deed, then I have no desire for a long life
Under such a reputation. For in no single care   510
The damage of this charge has brought me pain,
But in the general scope, if I should soon be called
A villain in the city, and an enemy of you and of my kin.

CHORUS

But surely this reproach came rather in his haste,
Constrained by rage, than in the wisdom of his knowledge.

CREON

But was it really claimed, that by mine own advice
The prophet was convinced to make a false report?

CHORUS

The things were said, but in what earnest
I do not know.

CREON

Did he with straight eyes and sound heart   520
Impugn me with this accusation?

CHORUS

I know not. For the doings of the great I do not see —
But he himself emerges from his home.

Enter OEDIPUS *from the palace*

OEDIPUS

It is you — how can you be here?
Or have you such a brazen face,
To come beneath my roof when you are known
For my assassin, and the proven thief of all my throne?
Come, tell me by the Gods,
Was it stupidity or fear you thought you found in me,
That you would plan to do such things?   530
That I would fail to note your work of stealthy treason,
Or that learning of it I would let it lie?

Or is yours not a mindless undertaking,
To attempt the throne without a following,
No crowds, no noble friends – a thing
Requiring money and support for its achievement?

CREON

Will you mark me? Against what has been said
Hear me in turn, and then judge, having learned my mind.

OEDIPUS

You are too eloquent, and I learn badly from you.
For I find your will toward me is cruel and heavy.   540

CREON

Now for the first time hear from me this very matter,
As I shall explain it –

OEDIPUS

'This very matter' do not tell me, that you are not false.

CREON

If you believe that stubbornness without reflection
Is a virtue, you are thinking crookedly.

OEDIPUS

If you believe you can betray a kinsman
And not answer for it, you do not think straight.

CREON

I agree, that is quite justly said –
But what these sufferings are, that you are said
To suffer at my hands – that you must teach me.   550

OEDIPUS

Were you or were you not convinced
That I should send for that pompous sage?

CREON [nodding 'yes']

And I am of the same mind even now.

OEDIPUS

How long is the time since Laius –

CREON

What has that to do with it? I don't have him in mind.

OEDIPUS

Since he disappeared, overborne by lethal force?

CREON

The long years of it reach far behind.

OEDIPUS
    Therefore this prophet was at that time practising?
CREON
    He was just as wise, and just as honoured.
OEDIPUS
    Did he mention me at all at that time?   560
CREON
    Not, at any rate, within my hearing.
OEDIPUS
    But you were powerless to find the killer?
CREON
    We made a search, but we heard nothing.
OEDIPUS
    Then how is it this wizard did not tell
    His version of it *then*?
CREON
    I have no idea. And I keep silent where I'm ignorant.
OEDIPUS
    If you're wise, you'll tell me what you know.
CREON
    Concerning what? If I know anything, I'll not refuse.
OEDIPUS
    Just this: that unless he had conspired with you,
    He never would have spoken of *my* having murdered Laius.   570
CREON
    If he said that, you must know about it. But I expect
    To learn as much from you as you now learn from me.
OEDIPUS
    Learn thoroughly; for I will not be taken for a murderer.
CREON
    Well then — are you not married to my sister?
OEDIPUS
    You ask about what no one would deny.
CREON
    And you rule the land with her, in equal power?
OEDIPUS
    Whatever she desires, I grant it to her.
CREON
    And with you both I do enjoy a third share of power?

OEDIPUS

  Yes, and given that, you seem the more spiteful as a traitor.

CREON

  But I am none, if you will reason it as I do.   580
  First examine this: would any man prefer
  To rule in fear, rather than to sleep at night at ease
  And have the selfsame power?
  For my part I had rather exercise
  The royal privilege, than be a king;
  And so would anyone who reasons prudently.
  For now I benefit in everything from you
  Without a care; but if I were king myself
  There would be much to do against my will.
  How on earth could it be sweeter to be king   590
  Than painlessly to share the rule, and 'prince' be called?
  I am not so confused as to desire
  Other honours than the useful, pleasant ones.
  Now I delight in everyone and all men bid me welcome;
  Now those who need you seek my intercession,
  For on it, all the fortunes of their enterprise depend.
  Why should I ever change my station for the crown?
  No sound mind would ever turn to treason;
  I have no love for such a policy,
  Nor would I have the gall to take another's part who did.   600
  And let this be the proof of it: go to Delphi,
  Discover for yourself what the oracle has said,
  And whether my report of it was right;
  Then if you find me in collusion with our soothsayer
  Kill me not by one vote, but join my own to yours;
  Do not condemn me on such cloudy inference.
  For it is not just, idly to suppose
  That evil men are honest, and honest men evil.
  For I think losing one good friend
  Is like the banishing of very life from one's own breast.   610
  But in time you shall know all my loyalty;
  For time alone reveals the virtue of a man,
  But his evil can be gathered in a single day.

CHORUS

  He has spoken well, cautious lest he fall;

For they are not secure who speak with haste.

OEDIPUS

When the contriving, secret rebel moves upon me swiftly,
I must swiftly make my stratagems in turn.
But if I wait in silence till his purpose be performed,
Mine own will all miscarry.

CREON

What do you intend? To banish me from Thebes?   620

OEDIPUS

I had rather kill than liberate you,
That you may show, for all, the meaning of pretension.

CREON

So you will neither test me nor believe me, speaking thus?

[*Oedipus shakes his head, 'no'. His line in the text here is lost*]

CREON

I see you are not in your right mind.

OEDIPUS

Oh, but I am.

CREON

But I must be sane myself.

OEDIPUS

But you are wicked by nature.

CREON

So you will agree on nothing?

OEDIPUS

And I must govern all the same.

CREON

Not if you govern madly.   630

OEDIPUS

O city, city!

CREON

I too share the city; it is not yours alone.

CHORUS

Stop, Lords! I see that none too soon,
Jocasta comes to you out of the palace door
With whom you must put right your present quarrel.

Enter JOCASTA, *crowned*

JOCASTA

O sorry men, why have you tried each other with bickering?
Are you not ashamed, dragging out your private grievance
While the country languishes in sickness?
Won't you return home, and you, Creon, to your chambers,
And no more magnify a petty cause?   640

CREON

Sister, your husband Oedipus decides
Which of two terrible punishments to put me to:
To be exiled from my country, or be put to death.

OEDIPUS

I affirm it, O my wife, for I have found him
Practising with treacherous designs
His spite upon our royal person.

CREON

May I never thrive, but be damned, – may I die,
If I have done the least of what you charge me with.

JOCASTA

O Oedipus, believe him by the Gods;
First in piety before his sacred oath,   650
And then for my sake, and for these your subjects.

CHORUS

Consent, take heed, and be wise, I beg you my Lord.

OEDIPUS

What would you have me grant?

CHORUS [indicating Creon]

That he, who never trifled with you in the past,
Be held in your respect, by this, his late sworn testimony.

OEDIPUS

Do you understand for what you ask?

CHORUS

I understand.

OEDIPUS

Then tell me what you mean.

CHORUS

That never on uncertain grounds should you condemn
To guilt and shame a friend who swears so gravely.   660

OEDIPUS

But understand this now: in seeking this,

You seek my exile and my death.

CHORUS

Not by the foremost God of all the Gods,
Not by the sun: friendless and godless may I die,
In uttermost despair, if ever I have such thoughts.
But the wasting country withers up my soul,
The worse if you should join
The evils of your discord to our older sorrows.

OEDIPUS

Then let him go, and if need be, rather let me die
Than be shamed in lifelong exile from my homeland.   670
For your mouth moves me to pity, though his cannot.
But while he is here, he shall be hated.

CREON

I see you are as bitter now as you were heavy
When your anger drove your heart so far.
And it is just, that natures like your own
Are most difficult for their bearers to withstand.

OEDIPUS

Now get thee gone, away from me.

CREON

I am leaving, and though you will not know me,
[*indicating the Chorus*] To these I am the same man I ever was.[49]

[*Exit Creon*

CHORUS

Lady, why do you delay, to bring your man inside the house?   680

JOCASTA

To learn what argument this was.

CHORUS

Ignorant suspicions rose from gossip,
And the wrong of it is ravenous.

JOCASTA

Did it come from both of them?

CHORUS

Yes.

JOCASTA

And what was the story?

CHORUS

It seems enough, with the land already sore,

To let the quarrel rest where it was left.

OEDIPUS

I see that you have come, though I know you mean well,
To merely trying to appease my heart.   690

CHORUS

My sovereign lord, I have not said this only once:
May you know me for insane, and set my mind at naught,
If ever I have yet rejected you,
Who have borne my dear homeland swiftly forward
With your labours, and now shall lead it into safety.

JOCASTA

By the Gods tell me also, my good Lord,
For what event you have upraised in you
So great an anger?

OEDIPUS

I'll tell you; for I reverence you more, Lady,
Than those who know it now.   700
The cause is Creon, and his designs against me.

JOCASTA

Explain, and clearly tell me all the fight from the beginning.

OEDIPUS

He claimed that it was I who murdered Laius.

JOCASTA

He said that by himself, or learned it from another?

OEDIPUS

No, by sending in the prophet
He left his own mouth free of any slander.

JOCASTA

Now put by you all the cares you speak of,
And hear from me, and learn
How no one among mortals truly has the art of prophecy;
And let me briefly show you all the proof of it: 710
The answer of an oracle once came to Laius –
I will not say it was from Apollo Himself,
But from the ones through whom He speaks –
That to Laius the fate would come,
That he be killed by his own child,
Whoever should be born from me and that king.
But as the tale is told, the man was murdered

By some foreigners, robbers at the crossroads
Where three trails come together.
And when our child was barely three days old,   720
Through the ankles of its feet he drove a little stake,
And in the hands of other men he sent it to the wilderness.
So here Apollo did not bear it out,
That the child should become the killer of his father,
Nor what so sorely frightened Laius,
That he be slaughtered by his son.
Thus did the prophecies scribble out their circles –
So do not vex yourself with turning through them.
For whatever needful thing the God seeks,
He Himself will effortlessly show it.   730

OEDIPUS

How my soul wanders back, woman,
And my spirit heaves, as I hear you speak.

JOCASTA

What sort of worry do you think on, saying that?

OEDIPUS

I thought I heard you say it, that Laius
Was slaughtered where three roads meet.

JOCASTA

Yes, that was said, and they still say it now.

OEDIPUS

And where is the place where he suffered?

JOCASTA

The place is called Phocis, and the set of roads
Goes out from Daulia and into Delphi itself.

OEDIPUS

And how much time has come and gone   740
Since this thing happened?

JOCASTA

It was about the time when you appeared in Thebes
And were proclaimed the ruler of the city.

OEDIPUS

O Zeus, what have You decided to do to me?

JOCASTA

But what is that to you, Oedipus, in your heart?

OEDIPUS

    Do not ask me. But tell me,
    To what age of his life had Laius come?

JOCASTA

    He was old, and the white had started growing in his hair.
    His face was not much different from your own.

OEDIPUS

    Oh my soul – wretched. I think that just now   750
    I have thrown myself under a grievous curse
    And did not know what I was doing.

JOCASTA

    What are you saying? My lord, I tremble looking on you.

OEDIPUS

    My heart quails, that the seer may not have been so blind.
    But show me better, and explain one thing more.

JOCASTA

    Though I shrink from it, when you tell me what it is
    I promise I will speak.

OEDIPUS

    Whether he left with just a few,
    Or many royal escorts to accompany the man?

JOCASTA

    In all they were but five, and among them   760
    Was a messenger. But Laius travelled in a single wagon.

OEDIPUS

    Oh, already all of it is proved!
    Who was it, woman, who told you these things?

JOCASTA

    A servant, the only survivor to return.

OEDIPUS

    And is he still here in the house, now?

JOCASTA

    Not at all. For when he came back from that place,
    And saw you reigning after Laius perished,
    He came and took me by the hands and begged me
    That I send him off into the fields, out to the sheepfold,
    So he could be as far as possible from sight of Thebes –   770
    And so I sent him. For I thought him such a worthy slave
    That he deserved at least that grace.

OEDIPUS

How can he be brought in haste back to the city?

JOCASTA

It is possible, but what do you want of him?

OEDIPUS

O woman, I am frightened for myself,
That I have said so many things
For which I need to see him —

JOCASTA

But he will come. And I hope I may be worthy,
O my Lord, to learn what thoughts you bear so heavily.

OEDIPUS

And that hope shall not be slighted: 780
I am so far gone — to whom can I speak but you,
As I move into a fate like mine?
Polybus of Corinth was my father,
And my mother Merope the Dorian.
I was held to be the greatest man
Of all that city, until something happened
Worthy of amazement, though not of all the tears
I gave it. Once at supper
A man who had drunk too much wine
Called me the 'counterfeit' son of my father.   790
And being burdened with that, I scarcely could restrain myself
All day, and next day I confronted both my parents with
                                            close questions —
And they were furious at him for his reproach, ·
The one who threw those words at me.
As for their explanation, I was so far satisfied.
But the thing still gnawed at me,
For the rumour of it spread.
So all in secret from my mother and my father
I made a journey into Delphi;
And Apollo, not honouring the questions I had come to ask,   800
Revealed to me the abject misery and terror of His word:
That I must be coupled with my mother
And show to mankind children that they find
Unbearable to look upon,
And become the killer of my father who begat me.

And hearing this, by the distant stars I gauged my way
To flee the land of Corinth, and seek exile
In some place where I might never see
Fulfilment of those miserable portents.
And travelling I came to those same regions   810
Where you say this king was killed.
And to you, woman, I will explain the truth:
I was walking near the triple-crossroads, and there came
A herald, and a man in a wagon drawn by colts,
Of the sort you spoke of, coming toward me
From the opposite direction; the driver
And the old man himself were bent
On throwing me from the road by force;
And the one who swore at me – that I must stand aside –
The driver – I struck him in a rage.   820
And when the old man saw me,
He watched for me walking close to his chariot
And beat me on the middle of my head with the sharpened rod
They use to goad the horses. I paid him back
In more than equal measure:
With a quick jab of my staff, from this hand
He was pitched down from the middle of the car
Onto his back, in a moment.
And I killed them all.
But if this stranger was related in some way to Laius,   830
Then who is now more wretched than this man? [indicating himself]
And what man more despised by spirits,
Whom no town, no stranger may receive,
Nor can any even talk to him,
But they must drive him from their houses.
And it was none but I myself who set this curse in place
To fall upon my head, – I defile the dead man's bed
With these hands by which he died;
Am I not evil? Am I not utterly unclean?
Now must I be banished, and when I go   840
I may not see my family, nor set my foot
Into my country, lest I be bound into a marriage
With my mother, and kill my father Polybus
Who begat me, and raised me –

And wouldn't one be right, to judge
That all this came upon me from a spirit
Cruel, and beyond the things of man?
Do not, do not, You sovereign holy Gods,
Let me see this day;
But let me vanish from the mortal world   850
Before a stain like this pollutes my life!

CHORUS

Your highness, we are frightened at these things;
But keep your hopes until you listen to the witness.

OEDIPUS

I have only so much hope
As makes me wait here for the shepherd.

JOCASTA

And when he has appeared, what will you do with him?

OEDIPUS

I'll teach you that — if he is found
Repeating your selfsame story,
I escape disaster.

JOCASTA

But what, of all you've heard me say,   860
Is so important to you?

OEDIPUS

You told me that the shepherd said
Laius was killed by thieves.
So if he still says it was *several*,
Clearly then, it was not I who killed him.
For one and many cannot be made equal.[50]
But if he says it was one solitary traveller,
Then the deed is already fallen on my head.

JOCASTA

But know that the story ran like so —
And he cannot contradict this —   870
I heard that it was many,
And I am not the only one who heard it thus.
But even if he sway from that report,
Never, O my king, will Laius' murderer
Be properly revealed to justice —
Since the oracle expressly said

That he must die at the hands of *my child*:
But that poor infant never killed him,
For he himself had perished long before;
So that where prophets are concerned,   880
I see their merit neither here nor there.

OEDIPUS

Well reasoned. But all the same,
Do not delay, but send a man to fetch the shepherd.

JOCASTA

I will send someone immediately.
But let us go inside the house.
For I will do nothing but what pleases you.

[*Exeunt Creon and Jocasta*

Third Choral Ode

CHORUS

May it be my portion to remain
In graceful purity of word and deed
Beneath established laws that walk on high
Begotten in the air of heaven   890
And only Olympus is their father,
Nor were they born from the race of men,
Nor shall Lethe ever close their eyes;
The God in them is great,
And they do not grow old.

Hubris breeds a tyrant;
Hubris, if it gorges on abundance
And in vain, against the moment and the circumstance
It mounts up to the highest,
Stepping from the precipice   900
To ruin, where the footsteps cannot help.
And I request it of the God,
That He never end our striving to be noble to the city.
I will never stop my reverence of God as our protector.

And if one should, in word or deed of hands,
Be proud and have no fear of justice,
Nor no awe before the statues of the Gods,
May some terrible fortune take him,

Cursed in his arrogance,
If he does not gain his profit fairly,   910
And puts by him pious ways,
To tamper recklessly with sacred things.
What man in such straits will boast
That he can shield his soul from the arrows of the Gods?
For if such acts are respected,
Why should I join in the dance and worship?

No longer will I go into the centre of all land
Praying at its sanctity,
Nor into the Abaian temple,
Nor Olympus, if these prophecies do not take hold   920
And teach by their example all the mortal race.
Therefore, O Ruler Zeus, Lord of all,
If ever You hear us clearly,
Let nothing go unseen
By You in Your eternal reign;
For now they slight the prophecies
Of Laius' legendary death,
And nowhere is Apollo given honour manifest,
But religion limps away.

Enter JOCASTA *from the palace as a suppliant, with wool and laurel*

JOCASTA
My lords of Thebes,   930
The thought came to me to betake myself
Into the temple of our household Gods,
Taking in hand these wreaths and incense.
For the heart of Oedipus rises to the height
Of every kind of pain; nor like a sane man
Will he compare new omens
To older ones that failed;
But the talker has his ear,
If he speaks of horrors.
And since my counsel can do nothing,   940
I have come to You, O Lycean Apollo,
Nearest God, as a suppliant with prayers,
That You might show us some solution
Undefiled by stigma.

For now we all are frightened,
Like the crew that sees its captain tremble.

Enter an old MESSENGER

MESSENGER

Can someone tell me, strangers,
Where is the house of Oedipus the king?
Or better, tell me where he is himself, if you know.

CHORUS

Beneath this roof, for the man is at home, Sir.   950
And the mother of his children is there also.

MESSENGER

And may she thrive in happiness and wealth,
Ever the mistress of that master's house.

JOCASTA

And the same happiness to you, Sir;
For your sweet words are deserving.
But speak, and tell us what you need,
Or what you've come to say.

MESSENGER

I bring good words to your house, and to your husband,
And to you, my Lady.

JOCASTA

And what words are those? From whom have you come here?   960

MESSENGER

From Corinth. And the speech I make will please you,
As how could it not? But perhaps it may trouble you –

JOCASTA

But what is it? And how can it have such double powers?

MESSENGER

The people of that land will have him for their king,
Of all the realm of Corinth, where they said this.

JOCASTA

Why? Does not the elder Polybus yet rule there?

MESSENGER

No more; for he is dead, and in the grave.

JOCASTA

What did you say? Has Polybus died, old man?

MESSENGER

    If I am lying, I deserve to die.

JOCASTA

    Handmaid! Go and quickly tell your master all of this.   970
    O you oracles divine, what are you now?
    Oedipus long ago fled from this man,
    Afraid lest he kill him – and now that same man
    Perishes not by Oedipus, but by gentle fortune.

Enter OEDIPUS *from the palace*

OEDIPUS

    O Jocasta, most beloved woman,
    Why have you summoned me from out my house?

JOCASTA

    To hear this man – and as you listen,
    Consider what those pompous oracles have come to.

OEDIPUS

    But who is this man, and what concerns me in his speech?

JOCASTA

    He comes announcing it from Corinth,   980
    That your father Polybus is no more;
    He has perished.

OEDIPUS

    What say you, stranger? Tell me again.

MESSENGER

    Since I must tell you this thing clearly first of all,
    Know well that the man has gone down into death.

OEDIPUS

    Was it by some treachery, or did disease break in?

MESSENGER

    A slight decline hath laid his aged body down.

OEDIPUS

    The patient man was killed by illness, I suppose.

MESSENGER

    And by the long measure of his years.

OEDIPUS

    Alas, my wife, why should anyone look to the shrine   990
    Of Pythia, or the shrieking birds who taught
    That I was bound to kill my father?

For he died, and he is hidden in the ground,
While for my part I did not touch a sword.
Unless he withered longing for my company.
But the prophecies, at least the ones we heard,
Polybus has taken down to Hades,
Where they worthless lie.

JOCASTA
And have I not said as much to you before?

OEDIPUS
You have. But I was led by fear.   1000

JOCASTA
Now brood no more upon them in your heart.

OEDIPUS
Must I not fear my mother's bed?

JOCASTA
Why should a man be afraid, for whom Nature rules,
And for whom no foreboding can be clear?
The greatest strength is but to live at ease,
As far as one is able. And you –
Never fear about your mother's marriage:
For already in their dreams have many mortals
Lain down with their mothers. But life is easy
For the one who sets such things at naught.   1010

OEDIPUS
All this would be well spoken of you,[51]
If my mother did not happen to be yet alive.
But as it is, since she lives still,
I still must fear, even if you speak well.

JOCASTA
But how great a comfort is your father's grave.

OEDIPUS
It is, I understand. But I do fear her,
Who still is living –

MESSENGER
Who is the woman who is so much to be feared?

OEDIPUS
Merope, who was Polybus' wife.

MESSENGER
But what is there in her that frightens you?   1020

OEDIPUS

A terrible omen that the Gods thrust down,
O stranger.

MESSENGER

Tell me, won't you? Or is it not for other men to know?

OEDIPUS

Just so. For Apollo told me
That I and my mother would be joined;
That I must take my father's blood upon my hands.
Because of that I long ago left my home of Corinth far behind.
And with fortunate result. But all the same,
It would be sweetest to my eyes
To look upon my parents.   1030

MESSENGER

And it was fearing these things
That you went to exile?

OEDIPUS

Old man, I needed not to be my father's killer.

MESSENGER

And have I not delivered you, great Lord,
From this fear, by coming here with good news?

OEDIPUS

Indeed you may take from me a worthy thanks.

MESSENGER

In fact, I rather came for that –
That when you come back home,
Some good may come to me.

OEDIPUS

But I will never go back to my parents.   1040

MESSENGER

O child, it's clear that you know not what you do.

OEDIPUS

How so, old man? Teach me, by the Gods.

MESSENGER

If you're afraid to come back home because of those things –

OEDIPUS

Yes, terrified lest Phoebus prove His word to me.

MESSENGER

Lest you take corruption from your parents?

OEDIPUS

Of just that, I shall be frightened forever.

MESSENGER

Do you realise that your worry is not justified?

OEDIPUS

How is it not, if I am the child of my parents?

MESSENGER

Because Polybus is no relative of yours.

OEDIPUS

What say you? Did not Polybus father me?   1050

MESSENGER [indicating himself]

No more than this man, but just as much.

OEDIPUS [indicating the messenger as he says 'no father']

And how can my father be no father?

MESSENGER

Ah, it was not I, nor that man, who begat you.

OEDIPUS

But — why then did he call me his child?

MESSENGER

From the time — know it — when he took the gift of you
From my hands.

OEDIPUS

And though this child had come from other hands,
He learned to love it so much?

MESSENGER

Yes, for his former childlessness won him over.

OEDIPUS

And did you buy me, or finding me by chance   1060
You gave me to him?

MESSENGER

I found you in the wooded gorge in the Cithaeron mountains.

OEDIPUS

Why had you made your way to such a place?

MESSENGER

I had set my flocks to graze there on the mountainside.

OEDIPUS

So you were a shepherd, and a wandering tradesman?

MESSENGER

And of you, child, I was the saviour, back then.

OEDIPUS

And what was my suffering, when you took me in your arms?

MESSENGER

Your ankles are the witness of that.

OEDIPUS

Ah me, why have you spoken of that old evil?

MESSENGER

I freed you, for there were spikes run through your feet.   1070

OEDIPUS

A dreadful shame I carried from the very cradle.

MESSENGER [*indicating Oedipus' ankles*]

So that from that fortune you are named as you are.

OEDIPUS

Oh, was it from the Gods, or my mother, or my father? Tell me!

MESSENGER

I don't know. But the one who gave you to me
Knows this better than I.

OEDIPUS

You did not find me yourself —
But had me from another?

MESSENGER

No, another shepherd gave you to me.

OEDIPUS

Who is he? Do you know him, to point him out
With some description?   1080

MESSENGER

He was surely called some servant of Laius.

OEDIPUS

Of the king of this country, long ago?

MESSENGER

Exactly. And this man was his shepherd.

OEDIPUS

And does he yet live, so that I can see him?

MESSENGER [*to the Chorus*]

You men of the country would know best.

OEDIPUS

Who is it of all you men present here
Who knows the one he talks of, having seen him
In the fields, or in this place?

Show it; for this is the moment
For it all to be discovered.   1090

CHORUS

I think it is no other than the man from the fields
Whom you lately sought to look upon.
But Jocasta might tell this matter best.

OEDIPUS

Woman, do you think this is the very man
To whom we lately sent command to come here?
Is that the man he speaks of?

JOCASTA

Why ask whom this man talks about? Do not linger on it;
And for the rest of what was said,
You need not deign but to remember it in idleness.

OEDIPUS

It could not happen, that taking evidence like this   1100
I should fail to show my origins!

JOCASTA

Do not by the Gods, if you care at all for your life,
Pursue this! I am aggrieved enough –

OEDIPUS

Take courage. For if I show myself descended
Of a mother who is thrice a slave,
Still *you* will not be baseborn.

JOCASTA

Still, obey me – I beg you. Don't do this.

OEDIPUS

I will not be persuaded not to learn it clearly.

JOCASTA

But I speak knowing too well what is best for you!

OEDIPUS

And your best advice enrages me again.   1110

JOCASTA

O damned one, may you never know who you are!

OEDIPUS

Someone go bring the shepherd here to me,
And leave this woman to rejoice in her nobility.

JOCASTA

O, O, you sorry, doomed man!

For that is all I can say to you,
And no other words ever again.

                              [*exit Jocasta into the palace*]

CHORUS

Why did she go, O Oedipus, the lady
Wildly racing from her pain?
I fear that evils will burst upon this silence.

OEDIPUS

Let break forth what must: 1120
But I will seek to know my origins,
However humble they shall be.
And perhaps milady, who lords it like a queen,
Is ashamed that I am ill-derived.
But I hold myself to be the child of Fortune,
Who has sometime blessed me,
And I shall not be dishonored.
For I am born from such a mother;
And the months, that are my brothers,
Have made me both a small man and a great one.   1130
So being born from such a parent,
I will never more be any other kind of man,
Nor fail to learn my lineage.

Fourth Choral Ode

CHORUS

If I am a soothsayer, wise in judgment and discerning,
By Olympus, it shall be you, O Cithaeron mountains,
That we shall glorify as Oedipus' nurse,
And his companion, and his mother,
On the next full moon; and we will dance for you,
Who brought such succour to our king.
And Apollo, to whom we cry, may these things please You.   1140

Which one, child,
Which of the long-lived Nymphs made love to Pan,
Roaming through the mountains, and begat you?
Or did Apollo's lover bear you?
For He adores all the wild highlands.
Or else Lord Hermes,

Or the God of Bacchanalian joy,
Dwelling on the heights of stone
Received the sweet surprise
From some nymph on Mount Helicon   1150
In whom He delights the most in dalliance.

OEDIPUS

If I must guess, even I who haven't dealt with him before,
Old man, I seem to see the shepherd
Whom we have been seeking.
He seems as aged as this man (*indicating the Messenger*)
And I recognise the ones that lead him
As my servants. But you will quickly overtake me
In that knowledge, having seen the man before.

CHORUS

Be certain of it, you are right.
For the man was in Laius' service,   1160
As trusted by him as any other herdsman.

Enter the old SHEPHERD

OEDIPUS [*addressing the Messenger and indicating the Shepherd*]
I ask you first, my guest of Corinth,
Is this the man you mean?

MESSENGER [*indicating the Shepherd*]
The very man you look upon.

OEDIPUS [*to the Shepherd*]
You, Sir, look at me, old man, look here
And answer whatever I ask you.
Did ever you belong to Laius?

SHEPHERD
I did. But not as a slave he bought,
For I was born in his house.

OEDIPUS
What labour had you? What kind of life?   1170

SHEPHERD
For the most part of my life
I have been called a shepherd.

OEDIPUS
What places had you for your neighbourhood?

SHEPHERD
I was in the Cithaeron Mountains,

And around there I was.
OEDIPUS
   And therefore, do you know of having met this man
   In that place?
SHEPHERD
   Doing what? And what man do you mean?
OEDIPUS
   This man right here. Have you ever had any dealings with him?
SHEPHERD
   Not to speak of, at the call of memory.
MESSENGER
   And it is no wonder, Master. But I shall awaken his
                                       forgetfulness   1180
   To lucid memory. For I am sure he does remember,
   When near Cithaeron, tending my one flock,
   I used to meet him as his two flocks grazed;
   This for three half-years, from each spring's beginning
   To Arcturus' rise in the autumn dawn.
   And when the winter came,
   I drove mine homeward to the sheepfold,
   And this man drove his back to Laius' pastures.
   Did any of these things happen as I say they did, or no?
SHEPHERD
   You speak the truth; but from a long time ago.   1190
MESSENGER
   Come now and tell me, do you remember giving me
   A child, that I might raise the foundling as mine own?
SHEPHERD
   What of that? Why do you ask that question?
MESSENGER
   Old friend, this is that one, who was an infant then.
SHEPHERD
   Go to ruin! Will you not be quiet, at last?
OEDIPUS
   Don't punish him, old man. Your words need punishing
   More than his.
SHEPHERD
   O most brave master, how have I done wrong?

OEDIPUS

   In not answering when this one asks about the child.

SHEPHERD

   For he speaks in ignorance, talking in vain.   1200

OEDIPUS

   If you will not speak from your free grace,

   You may yet from compulsion speak.

SHEPHERD

   No, by the Gods, don't torture me in my old age!

OEDIPUS

   Quickly – someone tie his hands behind him.

SHEPHERD

   For what? What else do you want to know?

OEDIPUS

   Did you give a child to this man,

   The child he asked about?

SHEPHERD

   I gave it. And I wish I had died that day.

OEDIPUS

   You will come to that pass yourself

   Unless you tell the honest truth.   1210

SHEPHERD

   I am likelier by far to perish if I speak.

OEDIPUS

   It seems this man is stalling . . .

SHEPHERD

   Not I, not at all. But I told you before,

   I gave the child away!

OEDIPUS

   Having taken it from where?

   From your own house, or from another's?

SHEPHERD

   It wasn't mine, I had it from another man.

OEDIPUS [indicating the Chorus]

   From what citizen, and out of what home?

SHEPHERD

   No, by the Gods, master, ask no more!

OEDIPUS

   If I ask you again, you are a dead man.   1220

SHEPHERD

He was a child of Laius' household.

OEDIPUS

A slave or some relative of his?

SHEPHERD

Oh, my soul! I am close to uttering the horror.

OEDIPUS

As am I to hearing it. But I must hear it still.

SHEPHERD

Indeed it was called a child of Laius.
But the woman inside, your lady, might tell it best –
For she is able.

OEDIPUS

Did *she* give it to you?

SHEPHERD

Yes, my Lord.

OEDIPUS

With what design?   1230

SHEPHERD

That I should do away with him.

OEDIPUS

The mother was so hard?

SHEPHERD

She was afraid of the predicted evils.

OEDIPUS

What kind?

SHEPHERD

The word was, that he would kill his father.

OEDIPUS

Then why didst thou give it to this old man?

SHEPHERD

From pity, Master,
Thinking he would take it to another country,
Where he came from. But he saved him –
And brought him thus into the worst of misery.   1240
For if you are the one he saved,
Know that you have been born to disaster.

[*Exeunt Shepherd and Messenger*

OEDIPUS

    Oh, Oh, it's clear, it's all happened!
    O light, I look upon you for the last time –
    I who have been shown
    That I am born from whom I must not be,
    Married whom I must not marry,
    And whom I must not murder, I have killed.

                  [*Exit Oedipus into the palace*]

Fifth Choral Ode

CHORUS

    O generations, nations of mortality
    How I do rate your lives at nothing: 1250
    For what man hath a fuller share of happiness
    Than the resemblance of it – and after semblance, ruin?
    And having you for mine example,
    Your fate, yours, wretched Oedipus –
    I call no mortal life a happy one.

    By prodigious skill,
    Oedipus shooting his arrow became
    The thriving master of every joy;
    O Zeus, he destroyed
    The riddle-chanting maiden with her twisted claws,   1260
    And he did rouse him like a tower
    Against the deaths she brought my country;
    [*turning toward the palace and speaking in the second person again*]
    And from that time,
    You have been called my sovereign,
    And honoured in the highest things
    Have you ruled in great Thebes.

    Whose lot is now more piteous to hear?
    Who lives among more savage hardship
    In the throes of misery, his life undone?
    O world-renowned Lord Oedipus,   1270
    How one great bed contained you
    That upon it you should fall
    As father, son, and bridegroom!
    And how did that place where thy father sired thee,

Wretched one, suffer thee in silence for so long?

Time that sees all
Has exposed you – in spite of you –
It passed sentence
Upon your marriage that is no marriage,
Wherein the getter of children   1280
Has so long been the child.
O son of Laius,
How I do wish I had never seen thee;
For I do mourn for thee as though
The dirges of the funeral were pouring from my lips.
To say it plain: from thee I drew a new breath of life once,
That now must close mine eyes again.

Enter PAGE *from the palace*

PAGE

O you ever-honoured ones of this great country,
You will hear of such deeds
And see such works –   1290
But take the grief upon yourselves
Like true-born Thebans of Labdacus' house,
For I do not think
The Danube nor the river Phasis
Could wash these houses to purity
But only cover and conceal them;
And the hidden, grievous works
Shall be exposed into the sun –
Deliberate ones, not accidents.
And those griefs hurt the most   1300
Which we discover we have brought upon ourselves.

CHORUS

What we were so afraid of
Cannot but be heavy.
But what do you say about those two? [*indicating the palace*]

PAGE

The soonest said and understood of all words:
Divine Jocasta is dead.

CHORUS

O poor, unhappy woman! By whose hand,

And how came her death?

PAGE

> She slew herself. But the bitterest of these deeds
> Is lacking yet – for you were spared the sight of it.   1310
> Still, so far as what my memory holds,
> You shall learn that woman's sufferings.
> For when, compelled by rage,
> She came inside the vestibule
> She threw herself upon her bridal bed,
> Beating her own head with both hands;
> And she came inside slamming the great doors,
> And called upon the long-dead Laius,
> And the memory of when she had his seed, long ago;
> By whose hand he was killed,   1320
> Leaving the mother to conceive
> Accursed children by the dead man's son.
> And she mourned for all her love, wherein
> Doubly undone, she had a husband by her husband,
> And children by her child.
> And how she died thereafter I know not.
> For Oedipus rushed in shouting
> That her grief was not for us to stare at;
> And so we stared at him pacing frantically,
> And he flew upon us crying for a sword   1330
> Demanding of us where he might find
> His wife that was no wife,
> The mother of himself and of his children.
> And then some demon showed her to him,
> For of all of us no man was near him then.
> But with a sudden scream, as if someone were guiding him
> He drove apart the double-doors,
> Breaking from their hollow pits the dead-bolt locks,
> And he fell into the bedroom.
> Wherein we saw his wife hanging by the neck,   1340
> Entangled in the twisted noose.
> And when he saw her, with a deep and miserable roar
> He untied the ropes, and when the poor queen lay upon
>   the ground –
> What came next was horrible to see;

For he unpinned the golden brooches from her robe,
The ones she always wore, and lifting them up high
He struck down into his eyeballs, to the sockets,
Screaming at them: that they would not see
The shames that he had suffered nor those he had performed,
And henceforth what he never should have seen   1350
Shall be in darkness, and what he longed for
He shall never know again. And chanting such things
Many times, and not just once, he struck and hit his eyes.
The holes were red, and his face was wet;
Nor did he bleed some few drops,
But like a dark rain, like hail,
He wept his blood. Oh, the old prosperity
They joyed in for so long before this moment –
It was a just and proper happiness.
But now, on this day,   1360
Moaning, rage, death, shame:
Such are the names of all their woes,
And there is none they lack.

CHORUS
    And what relief has the poor man now?

PAGE
    He calls for one to open up the palace doors
    And show to all of Cadmus' folk
    The patricide, whose mother is destroyed,
    He to whom it is unclean even to speak,
    That from this land they must banish him,
    No longer to remain here, a curse upon his house –   1370
    Just as he once commanded. But he lacks strength
    And needs someone for a guide;
    For the pain is unbearable.
    And he will show himself to you,
    For he opens the locks of the palace doors –
    And now behold a sight
    That you will hate . . . with sympathy.

                    Enter OEDIPUS, *blind, led by servants*

CHORUS
    O suffering, horrible for mankind to behold –

O most horrible of all that I have ever known –
What madness, sorry wretch, came over you?   1380
Which God is it, that from the farthest reaches
Leaps down upon your miserable portion?
Woe, woe, cursed one!
But I cannot look upon you,
Eager though I am, so much to ask of you,
So much to learn from you,
So much to see you –
You make me tremble so.

OEDIPUS

Aiai . . . aiai . . . I am so sad;
Where on earth am I brought in my misery?   1390
Where does this voice go, fluttering about me?
O my demon, where have you gone?

CHORUS

To the dire place, that cannot be heard,
And cannot be looked upon.

OEDIPUS

O my cloud of darkness,
From which I turn away,
Your coming-on is merciless, unspeakable,
And all-too-good for me.
Oh me! Oh me again!
Such piercing stabs   1400
And such a stinging memory of evils
Come into me all at once.

CHORUS

And it is not strange
That in such great anguish
You should doubly mourn that double loss you bear.

OEDIPUS

O Friend,
You are still my true companion,
For you still attend me in my blindness.
– Oh! –
For you don't forget me,   1410
And though I am in darkness
Yet I clearly know your voice.

CHORUS

 O you who have done terrible things,
 How did you endure the breaking of your eyes?
 Which of the Gods had set you on?

OEDIPUS

 It was Apollo! Apollo, O my friends –
 That brought my wicked sufferings to pass;
 But no one struck my eyes
 But I myself in desperation.
 But what need I see,   1420
 To whom the sight of nothing is a pleasure?

CHORUS

 These things are all exactly as you say.

OEDIPUS

 And what is there left for me to see,
 Or to love, or to talk with,
 That it might still be sweet to hear,
 O my friends?
 Get me out of here, quickly.
 Lead me away, my dear ones;
 I am the great pollution,
 The most vile man;   1430
 I am still among all mortals
 The one the Gods despise the most.

CHORUS

 O, sad in circumstances as in spirit,
 How I wish I never knew you!

OEDIPUS

 May he die, whoever he was
 In the wild nomad pastures,
 Who loosed my feet and saved me,
 Rescued me from murder,
 Doing nothing worthy of my thanks.
 For had I died then,   1440
 There would not be so much agony
 For me nor for the ones I love.

CHORUS

 Then I, too, wish this were so.

OEDIPUS

    I would not have come to be my father's killer
    And be called by men
    The husband of the one who gave me birth.
    But I am godless now,
    And an abomination as a son,
    Sharing a wife with the man
    Who begat me to my shame.   1450
    And if there is some older evil
    Deeper than all crimes,
    Oedipus is by his fortune such a one.

CHORUS

    I do not know if you have chosen well –
    For you would do better to be no more
    Than to live blind.

OEDIPUS

    Do not lecture me, that what I've done
    Is not the best course; advise me no more.
    For even if I yet could see
    I do not know how I should look upon my father   1460
    As I came into Hades,
    Nor upon my wretched mother,
    To whom I have done things more vile
    Than suicide could punish.
    And my children – born as they were,
    Was the sight of them dear to me?
    Never to my eyes, never again,
    Nor this town, nor its towers,
    Nor its sacred statues of the Gods –
    I, the most noble man alone   1470
    Of all the sons of Thebes – utterly undone,
    I renounce them all;
    I who commanded everyone
    To banish the unholy one,
    The one the Gods declared unclean,
    And a relative of Laius.
    And I, exposed with such a filthy stain as mine,
    Is it for me to look upon those things
    With lucid eyesight? Not at all.

But if there were a way   1480
To block the flow of hearing through mine ears
I would avail myself of that,
And stop up all my frame,
That I might be blind and never hear again;
For it is sweet to live in thought,
Away from the noise and flashing.
O Cithaeron, why did you protect me?
Why did you not take me and kill me straight,
So that I never showed myself to humankind
Nor whence I came? O Polybus and Corinth,   1490
And the country I have so long called my home,
How beautiful I was, as you raised me,
With such revolting sores corrupt beneath the skin!
For now I find myself a criminal born from crimes.
O three roads, and the hidden clearing
In the wooded glen,
And then the narrow passage to the triple crossroads;
My father's blood, that was mine own,
You roads drank at my hands!
Do you remember me at all?   1500
The things I did before you,
And then what followed when I came here?
O weddings, marriages, you make us;
And having made us you raise up again
The same seeds – and you have exposed
Fathers, brothers, children in a kinship of the blood,
Brides and wives and mothers
In the most shameful actions ever undertaken
By any mortal. But to speak is not the same
As never having done the ugly things;   1510
Therefore cover me and hide me somewhere
Far away, as fast as you can go, or murder me,
Or secret me away under the Ocean
Where you may never look on me again.
Go on, and deem a wretched man
Worthy to be handled – heed me,
Do not be afraid – for all my evils
Could not be borne by any other mortal than myself.

CHORUS

But your plea is timely now –
Creon comes here, to act and to advise;   1520
For he is the only guardian of the country
Left after you.

OEDIPUS

Oh me, what word shall we say to him?
What good claim can I make upon his trust?
For before now I denounced him as all base.

Enter CREON, with Oedipus' daughters

CREON

I have not come as a mocker, Oedipus,
Nor to revile your old mistakes,
[*to the Chorus*] But if the things of mortals do not move you,
Fear yet Lord Helios, whose flame sustains us all,
And do not tempt Him with the sight of such contagion,   1530
That neither earth, nor light, nor the sacred rain
Shall willingly receive. But with all haste
Get him inside the house.
For only kin may hear and see with righteousness
A kinsman's shame.

OEDIPUS

By the Gods, since you have swept away my expectations,
And come as a noble man, to me, the worst of men,
Obey me a little – for I speak to your concern
And not to mine.

CREON

And for what favour do you beg me so?   1540

OEDIPUS

Banish me from this land, as soon as may be,
To some place where I never shall be seen
Or spoken to by any mortal person.

CREON

I would already have done so –
You would have gone there well enough,
If it were not that I must learn first from the God
What must be done.

OEDIPUS

But that God's message is entirely revealed:
The patricide, the guilty one, me,
You must destroy.   1550

CREON

That was said, yes. But all the same,
Seeing in what great need we stand,
It is better to find out what must be done.

OEDIPUS

And will you ask the oracle,
On behalf of one wretched man?

CREON

Yes, for now even you
Might bring your trust to the God's word.

OEDIPUS

Aye, and now I lay this charge before you,
And I urge you on:
Raise up whatever burial mound you wish   1560
For her who is inside; for your own kin
Fulfil her final rites.
And may this my father's city never be condemned
To harbour me inhabitant while I live,
But let me dwell in the mountains
Where my Cithaeron is famous,
That my mother and my father chose
For my appointed tomb – so that I may die
The way they wanted, those two who planned to kill me;
And yet this much I know –   1570
I will not die from sickness,
Or any other cause of such a sort;
For I would not have been saved thus far from death
Unless it were for some enormous sorrow.
But let our fate come on, whatever it be.
For my male children, Creon, do not mind them;
They are men now, and they shall not starve
Wherever they may go, while their lives last.
But my poor, pitiable maiden daughters
Who have never sat at the supper table   1580
Without me there; who have shared in all

I have ever touched –
Take care of them for me. But first –
Let me embrace them, and weep our fill.
Come, my Lord. Come, highborn nobleman;
If I could touch them with my hands
It would seem to me as though I had them still,
As I did when I could see.
What have I said?
Or can it be that somehow by the Gods   1590
I hear my daughters weeping, and Creon,
Out of pity, sends me my darlings?
Have I spoken truly?

CREON

You have. For I arranged it,
Knowing their presence would delight you
As it always has.

OEDIPUS

And may you thrive – for this grace
May the God keep better watch upon your fate
Than He has upon mine.
O children, where are you? Come here, come   1600
Into thy brother's hands, my hands,
Whose work has brought about that these,
Thy father's once-bright eyes, should see this way.
O my children, I became your father
All unseeing, and unquestioning,
Where I myself was fathered.
And I weep for you. But I have not the power to see you.
I weep when I think upon your bitter futures:
What life you both must live out at men's hands:
For to what public gatherings, what festivals shall ye go, 1610
From which you will not homeward turn in tears
And miss the holiday? And when the time has come
When you are ripe for marriage,
Who will be the man? – who will run the risk, my children,
Of taking on this kind of stigma, that shall be
The burden of my children and of yours?
What evil is lacking? Your father
Slaughtered his own father; he made love

To her who bore him, even her out of whose body he was born,
And you were born from the same place,   1620
The same from which he had come –
Thus shall you be mocked. And then who will marry you?
There is no one, O my children, and it is certain:
Barren and unmarried you shall pine away to nothing.
[to Creon] Child of Menoeceus, you are the only father
They have left to them; for we who made them,
We are dead, the both of us.
Therefore, do not look on while these your kinswomen
Drift about as beggars, without husbands,
Nor reduce them to the level of my crimes;   1630
But have pity on them, seeing how young they are,
And withal how destitute,
Except for what your care may tender.
Nobleman, with your hand's touch give me your consent.
And to you, my children, I would have given much advice,
If your spirits were grown up enough,
But now pray for me this prayer:
That the right moment may grant you a life to live,
And you may come into a better life than your father's.

CREON
You have cried enough; come inside the house.   1640

OEDIPUS
I must obey, though it is not sweet.

CREON
For all things are noble at their proper time.

OEDIPUS
You understand the terms on which I take my leave?

CREON
You will tell me again, and hearing them I will know.

OEDIPUS
See that you send me out of the country, far from home.

CREON
The gift you ask of me is for the Gods to grant.

OEDIPUS
But I have become the one they hate the most.

CREON
Therefore your exile will speed well.

OEDIPUS

Then you agree to it?

CREON

I would not speak in vain what I did not intend.   1650

OEDIPUS

Then lead me away, now.

CREON

Let go of your children, and now walk away.

OEDIPUS

Don't take them from me!

CREON

Do not demand your will in everything,
For even your achievements have not followed you through life.

[Exeunt Oedipus, Creon, Page

CHORUS

Inhabitants of Thebes our fatherland, behold
This Oedipus that solved the famous riddle,
That was the man of greatest power,
Upon whom there was no citizen but stared
In admiring envy of his great good fortune;   1660
See, into what deadly waves of circumstance
He has come. Therefore, fixing our gaze
Upon life's final day, we shall call no mortal happy,
Until he cross the threshold of this life, free from pain.

OEDIPUS AT COLONUS

The Setting

Colonus, a place just over a mile northwest of the Acropolis of
Athens. In the background, the sacred grove of the Eumenides.
A rock is just within the boundary of the grove. The time is some
twenty years after the closing events of *Oedipus the Tyrant*.

Enter OEDIPUS *and* ANTIGONE

OEDIPUS

    Child of a blind old man, Antigone,
    To what fields have we come? Or to the city of which men?
    Who will receive the wandering Oedipus
    With meagre gifts this day?
    Those who beg for little, carry off still less;
    And this suffices me. My sufferings,
    And the long time I have lived with them,
    Have taught me to be satisfied: these, and third,
    My own nobility. But come child, stop
    If you see some place to sit, on unclean ground   10
    Or on the ground of the Immortals' sacred grove,
    And sit me down, that we may learn
    Of where we are. For we have come
    As strangers to the town, and we must do
    As we are told.

ANTIGONE

    Father, Oedipus who bear misfortune's burden,
    The towers that protect the city stand far off yet
    From my eyes; but this place here I do believe
    Is that holy garden, teeming with the laurel
    And wild olive and the vine: everywhere within,   20
    Countless feathered nightingales make sweet mouths,
    Singing. So bend your limbs upon this uncarved stone,

For you have walked a long road, for an old man.

OEDIPUS

Sit me down then, and guard the blind man.

ANTIGONE

If time and practice teach that, I have learned it.

OEDIPUS

Can you teach me where we are?

ANTIGONE

Athens I know, but not this spot.

OEDIPUS

So much, every pilgrim told us.

ANTIGONE

But this place here, shall I go off and learn of it?

OEDIPUS

Yes, child; find whether people live here.   30

ANTIGONE

But they surely do: no work is needed now, I think,
For I see a man nearby, approaching us.

OEDIPUS

Is he near here yet? Has he set out towards us?

Enter STRANGER

ANTIGONE

He is already come, and now the time is right
To speak what you will, for the man is here.

OEDIPUS

O stranger, from her who watches over me
I have heard that you have come, a guide propitious
To tell us what we do not know —

STRANGER

Before you ask the rest of it, come out
Of this grove: for on the ground you now hold,   40
None may walk.

OEDIPUS

What ground is this? To which God is it holy?

STRANGER

It is untouched, and none may live here:
For the fearsome Goddesses hold it,
Maidens of the Earth and of the Darkness.

OEDIPUS

Hearing what sacred name might I invoke them?

STRANGER

The All–Seeing Eumenides, our people call them.
But elsewhere They bear other mighty names.

OEDIPUS

Then may They welcome me graciously:
For I must not leave my seat upon this spot of earth.   50

STRANGER

Why is this?

OEDIPUS

The old oracle put me here.

STRANGER

Nor have I the heart to drive you out,
Until I tell the city what I do.

OEDIPUS

O by the Gods, my stranger, do me no dishonour:
I am such a beggar, and I turn to you in supplication
Saying so.

STRANGER

Demonstrate it, and fear no dishonour from me.

OEDIPUS

This country, wherein we have walked,
What is it called?   60

STRANGER

Listen, and you will know all that I know.
All of this place is holy. It is held by great Poseidon,
And the fire-bearing Titan, Prometheus, is within it.
The spot on which you stand is called the brazen threshold,[52]
Which guards Athens. And all the households of the place
Pray to him, the mounted horseman Colonus
Their founder, whose name they bear in common.
Not with words, O stranger, do we honour
Such places as these are, but by our life among them.

OEDIPUS

Then people dwell here, in this very place?   70

STRANGER

Yes, the power of the hero whose great name it bears.

OEDIPUS

Does someone rule them, or does discourse and debate
Fall to the people?

STRANGER

These are ruled by the king of the town.

OEDIPUS

Who is this man, who rules by words and strength?

STRANGER

Theseus he is called, the son of Aegeus before him.

OEDIPUS

Might one be sent from your number, to go to him?

STRANGER

To speak with him, and summon him, for what?

OEDIPUS

Conferring small favours, he may win great profit.

STRANGER

What profit from a blind man?   80

OEDIPUS

What we say, we shall unfold with insight.

STRANGER

Do you know then, stranger,
How you might do well? If indeed
You are noble, as you seem to be –
Stay here, where I found you
Until I speak of this with men
Who dwell here, not the men in town.
For they will judge concerning you,
Whether you must here remain
Or must go back again.   90

[*Exit Stranger*

OEDIPUS

Has the stranger left us, child?

ANTIGONE

He has, so that in silence, father,
You may speak all your mind,
And I alone am near.

OEDIPUS

O Virgin Women, faces marvellous,
Since in this land I now have sat me down

First upon a seat which is Your own,
To Phoebus and myself do not become unkind;
He who, when he was proclaiming all those many evils,
Told me of this, as of a respite after a long time: 100
When I come into my final country, I might find
A seat of the majestic Gods, Their stopping-place for strangers,
And turn the final length of life's long-suffering race,
My dwelling there a benefit to those who will receive me,
A ruin to my senders, who have driven me away.
And He promised it, that signs of these events should
                                                    come to me,
An earthquake, or some thunder stroke,
Or else the lightning bolt of Zeus.
Now I know that from your Majesties
Some faithful omen surely led me off the road   110
Into this grove. For otherwise
I would not have met You first –
I, a sober traveller, and You who take no wine[53] –
Nor sat me down upon this uncarved, sacred chair.
But grant me, O Ye Goddesses, the passage of my life,
Some closing of its course,
According with Apollo's word –
Unless I seem to You too slight for this,
I who must remain the slave of sorrows
Heaped the highest among mortal things.   Hear, O Sweet   120
Ones, children of the ancient Darkness,
Hear, thou city of the mightiest Athene,
That all men call most honoured Athens,
Take pity on this shadow of the wretched man,
This Oedipus; for this is not the man he was before.

ANTIGONE
   Quiet. Some aged men are come,
   Inspectors of your holy resting place.

Enter the CHORUS

OEDIPUS
   I shall be silent, and you lead me from the road
   And hide me in the grove, until I learn of them
   What words they speak. For in that learning   Lies the caution   130
   of our labour.

First Choral Ode

CHORUS

Look: Who was he? Where has he put himself?
The most insatiable of all, where has he fled?
Search for him, seeking him everywhere!
The old man is some wanderer,
And not of our own country,
Or he never would have entered
The untrodden orchard of those Girls divine, invincible,
Whom we tremble naming
As we pass it with averted eyes,   140
Not speaking, as we move the mouth
Of voiceless, thoughtful prayer.
But it is rumoured now,
That one has come who has no reverence for Them;
As I search throughout the sacred precinct
I cannot discern where he is hidden.

OEDIPUS

I am the very man.
For *I see by voices*, as they say.

CHORUS

Oh, Oh!
Terrible to see, and terrible to hear!   150

OEDIPUS

I approach you as a suppliant;
Do not regard me as a criminal.

CHORUS

Zeus Protector! Who ever is this old man?

OEDIPUS

Not a man of the best good fortune,
That any might congratulate me,
Elders of this land.
And I do show it.
Else I would not travel with another's eyes,
Nor tether my greatness to this little one.
[*indicating the child Antigone*]

CHORUS

Ah! Were you born blind then?   160

As it seems, your life has been
Both long and most unhappy.
But for my part, you shall not bring these curses on:
[*as Oedipus backs away, into the forbidden grove*]
You go too far, too far!
Luckless foreigner,
Lest you deeper stumble, in the verdant,
Sacred grove where none may speak,
Where the pouring water-bowl
Meets with honeyed streams of sweet libation,
Stand aside! Step out from it!   170
[*to themselves, despairing whether he has heard them*]
A great trail separates him from us.
Do you hear me, long-suffering pilgrim?
Will you bring us out some issue to discuss?
Step out from the untrodden place
To where custom suffers everyone to speak.
But first, keep silent!

OEDIPUS
O daughter, where in thought am I to go?[54]

ANTIGONE
Father, we must take care to do
Just as the townsfolk do,
And we must willingly obey such customs.   180

OEDIPUS
Touch me now.

ANTIGONE
Indeed I am.

OEDIPUS
O strangers, do me no injustice
Who am trusting you,
And parting from my safety.

CHORUS
Unless you quit these holy seats, old man,
Someone will lead you out unwilling.

OEDIPUS [*moving out*]
Is this enough?

CHORUS
Step further forward.

OEDIPUS

Further?

190

CHORUS

You woman, lead him forward,
Since you understand.

[*at this point three lines have been lost*]

ANTIGONE

Follow then, follow this way with your limbs of darkness
Where I lead you.

[*another lost line*]

CHORUS

Bear it, O unhappy one,
Stranger in a foreign country,
To hate what the city does not love,
And reverence what it loves.

OEDIPUS

Now lead me, child,
That walking out in proper piety
We may hold discourse and listen
Lest we fight against what must be.

200

CHORUS

Incline your step no further
From that ledge of natural rock.

OEDIPUS

Thus far?

CHORUS

Enough, I tell you.

OEDIPUS

Shall I sit down?

CHORUS

Yes, bending down and to the side,
Upon the surface of the stone.

ANTIGONE

Father, this is my charge.[55]

210

OEDIPUS

Oh me, oh!

ANTIGONE

Join your quiet step to mine,
Leaning your old body into my friendly arms.

OEDIPUS [*going limp*]
  Oh, my ruinous heartache.
CHORUS
  O sorry man, since you are at your ease now,
  Tell, what man were you born, among mortals,
  And as what labour-ridden wight are you led.
  And may I learn from what fatherland you come?
OEDIPUS
  O host, I have no country. But do not —
CHORUS
  What answer is this you make, old man?   220
OEDIPUS
  Do not, do not, do not ask who I am,
  Forbear and press no further in your seeking.
CHORUS
  What's this?
OEDIPUS
  A dreadful origin.
CHORUS
  Tell it.
OEDIPUS
  O my child, what am I to say?
CHORUS
  Whose seed are you, stranger,
  Tell us — and of what father?
OEDIPUS
  O me, what shall I suffer, my child?
ANTIGONE
  Speak, since indeed you step near the edge.   230
OEDIPUS
  I will speak: for I cannot hide it.
CHORUS
  You delay a long time — come to it.
OEDIPUS
  Do you know of a certain Laius?
CHORUS
  Oh! Oh!
OEDIPUS
  And of the race of Labdacus?

CHORUS
    O Zeus!
OEDIPUS
    And piteous Oedipus?
CHORUS
    Are you he, then?
OEDIPUS
    Take no fear from anything I say.
CHORUS
    Oh! Oh!   240
OEDIPUS
    Miserable one!
CHORUS
    Oh! Oh!
OEDIPUS
    Daughter, what shall we hit upon now?
CHORUS
    Out! Get you hence and quit the country.
OEDIPUS
    And what you promised? How will you fulfil it?
CHORUS
    No one need pay fortune's debt
    For doing what was done to him before.
    Lies are traded for deceptions,
    So that he gains not gratitude but painful labour.
    But you, back from these ancient seats,   250
    Move off, from out my country now
    Avaunt, lest you hang heavy needful business
    On my city.[56]
ANTIGONE
    O reverent-hearted strangers and hosts,
    Though you cannot abide my aged father,
    Hearing of his unwilled deeds,
    Yet heed me, for we supplicate you, O
    Hosts and strangers; take pity on us.
    On behalf of my father alone I beseech you;
    I beseech you, not blind in these eyes   260
    Wherewith I gaze into your own;
    But as if I came to you, a person of your own blood,

Choose for decency! We are in your power;
As upon the Gods do we wretchedly depend upon you.
But come, incline towards unexpected grace.
I ask you by whatever is dear to you of your own,
Either child, or bed, or debt, or God.
For you cannot find that mortal for the looking,
Who can escape, if God should lead him on.

CHORUS

But know, child of Oedipus,   270
We pity you equally for your circumstance.
Trembling before the God, I lack the heart
To speak, beyond what I have said ere now.

OEDIPUS

What good comes of it, to have acclaim
And reputation spread abroad in vain,
Since the Athenians, said to be the most religious people,
Possess the greatest power to protect and save
A suffering stranger, but what is this to me?
Since you expelled me from my seat,
And now you drive me out, afraid at my mere name?   280
Surely you do not fear my body, nor my actions.
For my deeds were things I suffered, more than things I did –
If I must speak to you of my mother and father,
On whose account you fear me – I know this well.
For how was I wicked, in my nature, who suffered
And retaliated? So that had I acted knowingly,
Even then I still should not be wicked.
Nor did I knowingly go where I went,
While they knowingly sought to destroy me,
At whose hands I suffered. And thus, O strangers,   I now 290
approach you by the Gods:
Since you made me stand apart, protect me.
And since you honour the Gods,
Do not slight Their portion. Consider that They see
The pious among mankind, and the impious They see,
And no escape has ever come, for an unholy mortal.
With the Gods' help, you might avoid concealing with a stain
The happiness of Athens, in unholy works;
But since you have taken me in my supplication,

Traded for your pledge, protect and guard me!   300
Nor dishonour me seeing my horrible face.
For I come a pious and a holy man
Bearing blessing for this town; and when the master comes,
Whoever is your leader, then will he hear it
And know all. But until then let no evil come.

CHORUS

Aged sir, your mighty arguments are many
And compelling, their words expressed
Not lightly. But the lord of this our land
Suffices us to reckon these affairs.[57]

OEDIPUS

And where is the commander of this ground,   310
O Xenoi? [58]

CHORUS

In the city of his father in this country. And that scout
Who sent me here, has gone to bring him.

OEDIPUS

Is he likely to consider me, and take thought
For a blind man, and come near me?

CHORUS

His Majesty will come,
When he learns your name.

OEDIPUS

And who is the messenger
To give him word of me?

CHORUS

The road is long. But myriad words   320
Love to wander up the way; take heart,
He will be here soon. For your name,
O elder, everywhere about
Is scattered far. Even if he rests now
At his leisure, when he hears of you
He will come quickly.

OEDIPUS

May he come with good fortune
For his own city and for me.
What noble man is not a friend to himself?[59]

ANTIGONE

O Zeus, what shall I say?   330
Where in thought am I to go, my father?

OEDIPUS

What is it, daughter Antigone?

ANTIGONE

I see a woman hurrying toward us
Mounted on a young Sicilian horse
And on her head a wide hat breaks the sun.
What shall I say? Is it she, or is it not?
Does my mind mislead me? I affirm and deny
And know not what I should say; wretched!
It is no other! At least
She greets me brightly with her eyes.[60]   340
She signals that she is alone; it is she,
Clearly, Ismene.

OEDIPUS

What say you, child?

ANTIGONE

I see your daughter, and my sister.
Soon we will be able to listen and learn.

Enter ISMENE

ISMENE

O father and my sister, sweetest to speak with,
I hardly found you; and now for my tears
I can hardly see you.

OEDIPUS

Oh, have you come, child?

ISMENE

To see you, O my poor-fated father!   350

OEDIPUS

Child, have you appeared?

ISMENE

Not without some hardship of my own.

OEDIPUS

Touch me, my child.

ISMENE

I grasp onto you both.

OEDIPUS

O common seed of blood . . .

ISMENE

O sorry nourishment of misery . . .

OEDIPUS

Her life and mine?

ISMENE

I shall be third in my own destitution.

OEDIPUS

Child, why have you come?

ISMENE

Taking thought for you, my Father.   360

OEDIPUS

You longed for me, missing me?
Or something else?

ISMENE

Yes, and by myself to make announcement to you,
With my only faithful servant.

OEDIPUS

Where are your brothers, who are young and for work?

ISMENE

They are wherever they are; this is their terrible moment.

OEDIPUS

Oh, how my sons make of their life and nature
All a perfect likeness of the ways of Egypt;
For there, men sit beneath the roof and work the loom,
While their partner women offer them always   370
The sustenance they win outside the home.
But in your own case, O my children,
Those who should have owned these labours
Keep at home like virgin girls, while in their stead
You toil through the evils of your father's woes.

[to Antigone]

For from the time when first you put off infant's food,
And were invested with a woman's frame and power,
You always shared a bitter portion of our wanderings
Leading your old man through many a wooded field
Bereft of grain, and barefoot; sometimes in teeming rains   380
And grievous heat of sunshine, braving exhaustion,

You held your own domestic comfort in contempt,
Second to your father's nourishment at need.
[to Ismene]
And you, child, who long ago carried
All those oracles, hidden from the Thebans,
To your father, all the prophecies that touched me —
As a faithful, trusted guard when I was driven
From my country. And now you come again, Ismene,
Bearing a message to your father? What errand is it
Calls you out from home? I well know you have not come   390
With empty hands, but you bring some terror for me.

ISMENE

I will let rest those sufferings I bore,
In search of your living and your whereabouts,
Lest I be doubly pained, labouring and telling of it.
About those evils which now befall
Your pair of dismal-fortuned sons —
About these I have come to tell you.
At first, it was their desire that the throne
Be left to Creon, in deliberation
Looking to the past of murder   400
In our family, lest it touch our city,
Having clung onto our house of pain.
But now, sinning in their hearts against the Gods,
They both have entered on a bitter strife, threefold:
To seize the rule and power of the tyranny.
The younger, being born but a little time behind him,
Hath robbed this elder Polyneices
Of his natural throne, and from his country
Driven him. To Argos valley he walked in exile,
And found new friends, allies who would bear his shield   410
Through alliance by new marriage, believing
That Argos should hold Thebes in reverence
And exalt its name to heaven.
These things are no handful of words,
O my father, but terrible deeds.
And I cannot learn precisely where the Gods
Shall have pity on your labours.

OEDIPUS

    Then you hope already that Gods
    Might somehow notice me, and save me?

ISMENE

    Yes, for I now convey to you these oracles,   420
    My father.

OEDIPUS

    What sort of oracles are these, my child?
    What has been divined?

ISMENE

    It shall be sought for by these men,
    That among them you should dwell,
    Before your death and after,
    For their benefit in their midst.

OEDIPUS

    How might they benefit from such a thing?

ISMENE

    Those oracles declare, that the power of those men
    Has come into your own hands.   430

OEDIPUS

    But I am no longer the man I once was.

ISMENE

    No. The Gods have corrected you, having destroyed you.

OEDIPUS

    How light a thing it is, to chasten an old man
    Who fell down young.

ISMENE

    And yet, understand me: not at length but in a moment
    Creon will arrive here at your side for this.

OEDIPUS

    What ever do they want me for, my daughter?
    Interpret this for me!

ISMENE

    In order that you may stand nearby the Theban ground,
    And the virtue[61] of your presence make them strong: 440
    But that you keep from entering their border.

OEDIPUS

    What help could I be, from beyond their gates?

ISMENE

   Your heavy tomb will bear ill fortune for them
   If they neglect the rites they owe it.

OEDIPUS

   Someone might suppose this much, even without the God.

ISMENE

   For the sake of this service, they are willing
   To make you an ally, near to the country,
   Lest you dwell somewhere under your own power.

OEDIPUS

   And will they cover me in Theban ashes for my burial?

ISMENE

   They would disallow you that, for your blood-guilt,   450
   O my father.

OEDIPUS

   Then they shall never have power over me.

ISMENE

   In the future, Cadmeans will feel the weight of this.

OEDIPUS

   In what sort of circumstance, child?
   How evident?

ISMENE

   Through your anger, when they stand before your tomb.

OEDIPUS

   Who told you this, which you now repeat?

ISMENE

   From men who witnessed at the Delphic shrine.[62]

OEDIPUS

   And Phoebus spoke of me, and touched on these things?

ISMENE

   So they said, who came through the plain of Thebes.   460

OEDIPUS

   Has either of my sons heard this much?

ISMENE

   They both have heard alike, and understand it well.

OEDIPUS

   And then, the worst of men had heard of this already,
   And they yearned more for the tyranny than for me?

ISMENE
   I suffer hearing so, but I must bear it.
OEDIPUS
   May the Gods not provide
   The quenching of this strife,
   But let it come down to my judgment,
   The fight between the two of them
   Wherein they now take up the spear: 470
   That neither him who now controls
   The sceptre and the throne should keep them,
   Nor should the exiled one be taken back,
   Though he dearly wish it. For they,
   Though begot by me, thus dishonored me,
   When I was driven from my fatherland,
   Who neither harboured me nor intervened,
   But I was made to stand aside, announced
   An exile. You might retort
   That exile was my wish, in those days,   480
   A gift the city properly granted me.
   No indeed: at that time, just after
   My undoing, in my seething anger
   Sweetest to me was to die, by stoning.
   No one appeared, to help me in that wish.
   But in time, all my hardship ripened
   And made mild, I learned how my heart
   Had run beyond all boundaries, ignorant;
   Too harsh a judge of my own past
   Mistakes. But at that time, by force the city   490
   Drove me from the land, and my sons,
   Though they had power to help their father,
   Were willing to do nothing, and for lack
   Of some few words in my defence,
   I was driven out, to beg in exile forever.
   But from these two girls, yet young virgins,
   I derive my nourishment and life,
   So much as nature gives it them.
   A bit of ground with no fear, the shelter of kinship.
   But the brothers, in their nature opposite,   500
   Have exchanged me for a throne,

To win the sceptre and their country's tyranny.
But they will not gain this ally, nor ever
Any blessing of their rule at Thebes.
I know it, when I bring to mind the oracles
This girl has heard, and those fulfilled
By Apollo from the past, reposed in me.
So let them send Creon to bring me,
And whoever else has power in the city.
And if, my hosts, you should be willing   510
To support me, strengthened by those Goddesses,
Divine protectors of the people: then
You will raise up for this city a great saviour,
And for my enemies a painful labour.

CHORUS

You and these two girl children of yours
Are worthy of pity, Oedipus: and since
You offer yourself as saviour in this speech,
I wish to offer you advice
About our circumstances.

OEDIPUS

O dearest ones, be the patrons of a stranger,   520
Sure that presently I shall fulfil it all.

CHORUS

Now put on such cleansing as you owe
To those divinities whom first you came upon.
You have been treading on their ground.

OEDIPUS

By what manner?[63] Teach me, hosts and strangers.

CHORUS

First take libations sacred from that ever-flowing stream,
And bring them, touching water with your cleansèd hands.

OEDIPUS

And when I have this pure stream's water?

CHORUS

There are krater-bowls, works of skilled men;
You must crown them with wreaths of wool   530
Upon the handles run around their mouths.

OEDIPUS

Twined with young branches? Or how braided?

CHORUS

Take the new-shorn fleece of a young ewe.

OEDIPUS

Very well. And after that, how do I end the rite?

CHORUS

Stand eastward, toward the source of dawn
And pour libations.

OEDIPUS

Pour libations with these vessels? The ones you spoke of?

CHORUS

Yes, a threefold pouring. Pour the last bowl empty.

OEDIPUS

When I have placed the bowl, with what shall I fill it?
Teach me that, too.   540

CHORUS

With honey and with water: use no wine.

OEDIPUS

And when the shaded ground has taken these?

CHORUS

Lay thereon three times nine saplings of the olive
With each hand, while you unfold the prayers.

OEDIPUS

I want to hear these prayers. They are the most important.

CHORUS

You whom we call Eumenides, Kind-hearted Ones,
With kind hearts receive my supplication to be saved.
You must pray thus, or thus must some other pray for you;
Quiet your voice so that you are not heard, and shout not.
Then step back again, and do not turn about.   550
Take courage and do these things: then I shall stand by you.
But if you do aught otherwise, then I should fear for you
                                                terribly, stranger.

OEDIPUS

Daughters, have you heard these men, who dwell nearby?

ANTIGONE

We heard. And he who does these things
Must do whatever is commanded in them.

OEDIPUS

This is impossible for me; let me be left behind,

For I lack strength, and I cannot see: a pair of faults.
One of you two, go and perform all this.
For I believe that in these rites, one soul
Will be sufficient, capable to pay   560
The debt owed by a myriad, if she goes
Mindfully to the shrine. Do it, my daughters,
Set to it quickly, but do not leave me behind
Alone. For my body is not strong enough
To follow after, and I have no second guide.

ISMENE[64]

I myself shall bring this to pass.
But I must find the place, and want to learn it.

CHORUS

It lies beyond the grove, guest. A resident is there,
If you lack for anything; he will direct you.

ISMENE

I shall go off and do this. Antigone,   570
Guard our father here. For to the children,
If some labour falls, they must not count it labour.

Second Choral Ode

CHORUS

Fearsome are the evils long since laid down,
O stranger, and their awakening to memory.
And yet I yearn to ask you.

OEDIPUS

What is it?

CHORUS

I would learn of that suffering you endured
Which proved to have no cure.

OEDIPUS

It is not proper to your hospitality,
To broach those shameless sufferings of mine.   580

CHORUS

Your story is rumoured far, and the telling
Will go on. I need to hear it straight.

OEDIPUS

Oimoi.[65]

CHORUS
 Consent, I pray you.
OEDIPUS
 Pheu, Pheu.[66]
CHORUS
 Be persuaded. Even as I was of use to you.

OEDIPUS
 Indeed, then, strangers, I bore the most evil thing,
 And God knows I bore it unwilling;
 Not at all self-chosen that way.
CHORUS
 But how so?   590
OEDIPUS
 Through evils of the bed, the city bound me –
 All unknowing, in a marriage of ruin.
CHORUS
 Was it as I hear, that from your mother
 You came to fill her bed, and earned a bitter name?
OEDIPUS
 Oh me, it is like death to hear these words,
 O strangers! But those two girls, who came from me –
CHORUS
 What say you?
OEDIPUS
 Children, and two downfalls!
CHORUS
 O Zeus!
OEDIPUS
 I was born from the pangs of the same mother.   600

CHORUS
 And yours are descended from you, and from . . .
OEDIPUS
 Yes, I am their brother, with a mother in common.
CHORUS
 Oh!
OEDIPUS
 Oh, indeed! Myriad, teeming, returning evils!

CHORUS

You have suffered.

OEDIPUS

I have suffered unbearably.

CHORUS

You committed acts.

OEDIPUS

Yet I did nothing!

CHORUS

How then –

OEDIPUS

I accepted the gift, that I wish I never had Taken from the city 610
in return for my service.

CHORUS

Miserable man! What else then?
Were you accustomed to bloodshed?

OEDIPUS

You really want to learn it?

CHORUS

Your father?

OEDIPUS

Ah, you have dealt me one more blow,
Disease upon disease!

CHORUS

You killed.

OEDIPUS

I killed. But to me –

CHORUS

What's this? 620

OEDIPUS

The deed has justice in it.

CHORUS

How so?

OEDIPUS

I will explain it. Even if I did,
Those whom I killed would otherwise
Have destroyed me. And I am pure in law:
I entered that fight in total ignorance.

Enter THESEUS

CHORUS
  Here now our King, Theseus, Aegeus' seed,
  At your call, to perform his needful office.

THESEUS
  I have recognised you, having often heard ere now
  Of that murderous destruction of your eyes;   630
  Of your coming now, child of Laius,
  I heard rumours in the road,
  And now I know it better still. You show us
  By your dress and sorry face of scars
  That you are he; and in pity for thee
  I would ask, ill-fortuned Oedipus,
  What it is for which you do present yourself
  To me and to our city, you and your unfortunate
  Companion. Teach me. It would be some prodigious tale
  Of deeds, that *you* could tell: such as I shrink from.   640
  For I know that just as I myself was by a foreigner
  Raised in exile like your own, so you, more than any other man,
  Come from foreign places. I have contended at great risk
  To my person, so that there is no stranger such as you are now
  Whom I would turn away, if I might bring salvation.
  For I well know, that being but a man, my portion
  In the future is no greater than your own.

OEDIPUS
  Theseus, your nobility has spared me,
  So that I need only speak in brief
  For a moment. For you have rightly named   650
  Who I am, and of what father sprung,
  And what country I came from;
  There is little needful left for me to say
  Before our talk is done.

THESEUS
  Teach me this now, so that I learn it all.

OEDIPUS
  I have come to give you the gift
  Of my suffering body: meagre to look upon,
  Oh but the profit of it far excels a lovely shape.

THESEUS

> What kind of profits do you prize thus
> And claim to come bringing?   660

OEDIPUS

> You shall learn that in time,
> Though not quite yet.

THESEUS

> When will your gift be shown?

OEDIPUS

> When I have died, and you have given me burial.

THESEUS

> You ask for what comes last in life,
> Neglecting all between, as of no worth.

OEDIPUS

> Yes, for all between is gathered up in this.[67]

THESEUS

> You ask this grace in but a few brief words.

OEDIPUS

> Yet look to it: my struggle is no small one.

THESEUS

> Do you mean the struggle of your sons,   670
> Or some other, that concerns me?

OEDIPUS

> They need me, my King,
> And they would bring me there.

THESEUS

> If they wish to bring you and you wish to go,
> Then exile is not right for you.

OEDIPUS

> They did not consider my wishes,
> Nor allow me them.

THESEUS

> But anger amid evils, foolish man, is useless.

OEDIPUS

> Warn me when you have heard my story;
> For now, allow me.   680

THESEUS

> Teach me. For without your view
> I should not speak.

OEDIPUS

Theseus, I have suffered terribly:
Evils upon evils.

THESEUS

You speak of the old days of your family?

OEDIPUS

Not at all: that matter, every Greek
Has shouted of aloud.

THESEUS

What misery is this, that lies beyond
All human grief?[68]

OEDIPUS

It is thus with me: from my homeland   690
I was driven out, by my own children.
And it is not mine ever to return,
For this: I have killed my father, long ago.

THESEUS

How then will they send for you, so that you dwell apart?

OEDIPUS

The mouth of the God has compelled them.

THESEUS

What sort of terrible suffering threatens
In this dread compulsion?

OEDIPUS

That they must be struck down upon this ground.[69]

THESEUS

How would bitter enmity arise, between my city
And those men?   700

OEDIPUS

O dear child of Aegeus, only to the Gods
Do death and aging never come; but all things else
Consuming time destroys. It withers the power of the earth;
It withers the body; and whereas it kills faith,
It brings the lack of faith to bloom, and the spirit
Is never the same that obtains between dear friends,
Or city and city. For some already, and others in the future,
The sweet joys turn to bitterness, then back again to love.
As for Thebes, even if she pass this day in peace with you,
And a myriad of myriad days and nights be born,   710

In which the present circumstances are resolved
Into a pledge of friendship, she will,
Upon some petty cause of words,
Scatter her pledge into the wind:
So that my sweetly sleeping, hidden corpse
Will drink their hot blood,
If Zeus is Zeus still, and His son Apollo, wise.
And though it be not sweet to hear these words,
That should be still, allow me to leave off
Where I began: and you on your part,   720
Only keep faith with me, and you shall never say
You welcomed Oedipus to this place and did not benefit:
Unless the Gods are lying to me.

CHORUS

Sovereign, even now this man declared himself
Ready to perform these same things and their like
Upon our ground.

THESEUS

Who indeed would reject the grace of such a man,
Who from the first has been a spear-friend,
When our common cause has always been the grace
Of hospitality? And since this godly suppliant   730
First arrived upon our grounds, he has given me
No trivial portion of honour. For which,
Being pious, I shall expel him never,
But establish him, a dweller in our country
And a citizen. And if it should be sweet to our guest
To remain here, I charge you with guarding him.
But if you prefer to walk with me, Oedipus,
I grant the choice to your own discretion.
For in this matter, I will take your part.[70]

OEDIPUS

O Zeus! Be good to such a man as this!   740

THESEUS

What do you need? Will you come with me
To my home?

OEDIPUS

I would if it were proper. But this is the place —

THESEUS

    Where you do . . . what? I shall not oppose you.

OEDIPUS

    Where I shall overpower them, who have expelled me.

THESEUS

    This would be the grand benefit you spoke of,
    From your dwelling on this spot.

OEDIPUS

    And it shall be, if you will keep your word
    You gave me.

THESEUS

    Take heart from me, sir: I will not betray you.   750

OEDIPUS

    I will not tender you my trust
    As I would unto a wicked man,
    Under an oath.[71]

THESEUS

    That oath would bring you no more than this word.

OEDIPUS

    Then how will you behave?

THESEUS

    What, precisely, gives you pause?

OEDIPUS

    Those men will come.

THESEUS

    But these men will be here to consider them.

OEDIPUS

    Be circumspect in leaving me.

THESEUS

    Do not teach me what I must do.   760

OEDIPUS

    My fear compels me.

THESEUS

    Have no fear in your heart on my account.

OEDIPUS

    You do not know what threatens.

THESEUS

    I know that no men will oppose my force
    And lead you out of here. Many vain threats

Are given words in anger. But when the mind
Masters itself again, threats come to nothing.
If indeed the courage has befallen them
To boast of your supposed extradition,
I know this: that brief route overland   770
From here shall seem impassable
As is the open sea. Now would I have you take courage:
Even without my protection you would yet be safe,
If Phoebus has sent you here. And thus I know,
That even if I were not here, my name alone
Would guard you from grievously suffering.

                                                        [*Exit Theseus*

Third Choral Ode

CHORUS
Great-horsed is this greatest land, O stranger;
You have arrived at the land of the Earth's strongest home:
This is pale Colonus, frequented by the yellow-green
Trilling songbird, deep in wooded glens;   780
Ivy grows here, wine-dark,
In the untrodden precinct of the God,
Teeming even in winter with myriad fruit
On shady leaves, in all the winter winds;
There steps the Bacchanalian immortal
Dionysus among the Goddesses who raised Him.

Here grows the abundant, lovely clustering narcissus
Bedewed each day by heaven, perpetual;
Ancient crowning garland of the great two Goddesses[72]
And the gold shimmering crocus.   790
Nor do the springs of Cephesus river fail,
Wandering in streams, but always and each day
It brings its quickening rainfall through the plain
Hastening what grows in the mighty earth with waters pure.
Nor have the choiring Muses turned from here in hatred;[73]
Nor has the gold-reined Aphrodite.

And there is something there such as I never heard
To grow on Asian ground, nor on the great Doric

Peloponnesian island: a teeming shoot
Untouched by human hands, and self-renewing,   800
The terror of raiding spearmen, which grows
Mightily in this land: the blue-gray, child-nurturing olive tree
Which neither youth nor commanding elder will wreck
With a destroying hand, but always Zeus the Protector,
Even blue-gray eyed Athena, keep watch about it.

I have another matter for my praise to tell:
This strongest mother-city, gift of the great Divinity,
A blessed country, abundant with great horses' glory
Abundant with foals, near the abundant ocean,
O Son of Cronos, for it is You who have thus   810
Blessed her, Lord Poseidon; with the healing bridle
You first bred great horses for these roads
And filled the rowers' hands with the well turned oar
That leaps upon the fearsome ocean, following
The Nereids' hundred-footed dancing crowd.

ANTIGONE
O land most praised with prayers,
Now should your bright words shine out indeed.

OEDIPUS
What news is it, my child?

ANTIGONE
Creon approaches us here, not without henchmen,
Father.   820

OEDIPUS
O most dear elders, please show me out
From among you, and now make good
My sanctuary.

CHORUS
Take courage; it will be. For even if I am
An elder, this land's strength has not aged!

Enter CREON, *with armed guards*

CREON
Resident noblemen of this country, I see
Some new fear in your eyes has taken you
At my entrance here; but do not shrink from me,
And let no evil word from you proceed.

For I have not come here wanting to perform   830
Some feat, since I am an old man, and I know
The city to which I have come is strong,
If any Greek city is; greatly. But I come
Sent here, aged as I am, to persuade this man
To follow me back to the plain of Thebes;
Sent not by one man, but under the command
Of all the population of the town: it fell to me
Because of kinship, to lament his sorrows more
Than any other citizen. Still, poor Oedipus,
Hear me: come home. The whole Theban people   840
Justly calls upon you, and I most of all, as I –
Unless I am born the most evil of human beings –
I suffer your evils, old man, beholding you as you are,
A wretched exile, ever the wandering vagrant,
Dependent on your only guide, travelling with nothing
To sustain your life. I for my part had not thought
That this poor wretch would fall so deep into misfortune
And indignity, as it would seem she has,[74]
The wretched girl; tending always to your sorry head,
A beggar at her age, with no livelihood,   850
And no experience of marriage, but she may belong
To the first one who finds her! This is a horrible reproach,
Is it not? I have degraded myself, and you and all our household,
Have I not? But there is no one to hide this manifest shame,
So you, now, by the Gods of our fathers, Oedipus,
Be persuaded by me to hide it: come willingly
Home to the town of your fathers, having addressed
This dear city.[75] For it is worthy. And yet full justly
Must the Theban homeland hold your reverent fear,
Being the place of your growth, from long ago.   860

OEDIPUS

Thou all–daring man, always ready to derive
A complex scheme out of a righteous case!
Why do you try me a second time,
Seeking to ensnare me with those same affairs
By which my capture would afflict me most?
For in the past, when I was ill with my own
Household evils, when I craved exile

From the land, you were unwilling,
Lacked the grace to grant me what I willed;
But when my anger over that was satisfied,   870
And my sweetest remedy was supper in my home,
Then you wanted to cast me out, and banish me: *then*,
That 'kinship' had nothing whatsoever of familial love.
And now again, as you perceive the harmony of mind
Between myself, this city, all its people, and its king,
You try and drag me back, speaking hard things softly.[76]
And what pleasure is in this, to be loved unwilling? [77]
It is as if a man had given you nothing, though you persisted;
And was unwilling to equip you, though your heart were full
Of yearning for what you required; then, he might give: 880
When the grace of it can bring no grace, this would be
Satisfaction in vain, would it not?
Such as you tender to me now,
In these noble words, these deeds of garbage.
And I will tell these men as well, so that I may show
Your fraudulence: you came here to lead me off,
Not into your home, but you would settle me
Dwelling nearby, so that your city escape unharmed
From the scourges of this country's men.
Not for you, such things, but *this* is yours, instead: 890
My avenging curse, dwelling in the land forever:
And this is for my sons: to gain only
So much of my land as they may die on.[78]
Do I not reckon Theban affairs
More wisely than you? By far, and by so far
As the sources where I listen are more wise:
Phoebus, and even Zeus, who is His father.
You arrive here with your flattering, cozening mouth
That keeps so many bladed edges hard:[79]
And yet by all your arsenal of words you will win   900
By far more evil than salvation. Even so, I know
I have not persuaded you of these things. Go.
And let us live here: for that is no misfortune,
Though we live but as we are now, if only
We accept it.

CREON

    Is it you, or I, who suffers most
    By your position in our present talk?

OEDIPUS

    It is sweetest to me, if you fail to persuade
    Me and these men near me.

CREON

    O poor unfortunate, shall it be shown   910
    That even time has not provided you with wisdom,
    But you survived to put a stain upon old age?

OEDIPUS

    A clever tongue you have. But I know no man
    Who speaks well everywhere, on any and all occasions,
    And yet is just.

CREON

    Saying what fits and continuous talk
    Are different things, and far apart.

OEDIPUS

    You believe you spoke your own words briefly,
    At the proper time!

CREON

    Not at all, for anyone whose mind is like your own.   920

OEDIPUS

    Go. And I will say it for these men as well:
    See that you make no move to trail or shadow me
    Here where I must make my dwelling.

CREON

    Not you, but these men,[80] I call to witness:
    As for your exchange of words with me,
    And the friends I represent, if I ever do take you –

OEDIPUS

    And who could take me, against the wishes of such allies?[81]

CREON

    I tell you, you will soon be aggrieved, even without that.

OEDIPUS

    What deeds are you threatening in those words?

CREON

    I have just sent for one of your two daughters   930
    To be extradited; the other I will lead off soon.

OEDIPUS

   Oimoi.

CREON

   Soon you will have more to groan about than this.

OEDIPUS

   You have my daughter?

CREON

   And this one too, before long.

OEDIPUS

   O my hosts! What will ye do?

   Or will you betray me, and not expel

   This unholy man from out your country?

CHORUS

   Away, stranger, go quickly;

   For you do not do justly now, nor were you just   940

   In what you did before.

CREON [*to Guards*]

   It befits you to take her unwilling now,

   If she will not come willingly.

ANTIGONE

   Oh me, wretched girl! How shall I escape?

   What help can I expect from Gods or mortals?

CHORUS

   What are you doing, stranger?

CREON

   I will not touch that man,

   But her, who is mine.

OEDIPUS

   O lords of the earth!

CHORUS

   O stranger, you do an injustice!   950

CREON

   This is justice.

CHORUS

   What justice?

CREON

   I lead away my own.

OEDIPUS

  O, city!

CHORUS

  What do you do, stranger?
  Will you let her go?
  We will quickly come to blows.

CREON

  Back off!

CHORUS

  Not from you, while you intend this.

CREON

  Vex me at all, and the cities will fight.   960

OEDIPUS

  Did I not predict all this?

CHORUS

  Unhand the girl, quickly!

CREON

  Make no demands where you lack the power.

CHORUS

  Let go, I tell you!

CREON

  And I tell you: step off![82]

CHORUS

  Step up, thus! Advance, ye dwellers at Colonus; advance!
  The city is attacked, our city, attacked by force! Advance
  With me, thus!

ANTIGONE

  I am dragged away wretched! O my hosts! My strangers![83]

OEDIPUS

  Where, my child, tell me!   970

ANTIGONE

  They take me by force!

OEDIPUS

  Reach out your hands, child!

ANTIGONE

  But I have no strength!

CREON [to Guards]

  Won't you lead her off!

              [Exeunt Guards with Antigone and Ismene

OEDIPUS

Oh, I am wretched, wretched!

CREON

These two crutches shall never more sustain your steps:
But since you yearn for victory over your fatherland
And friends, under whose orders I have done these things,
Though a prince of the royal house, prevail then.
For I know this, as in time you shall know it too: 980
You acted nobly neither now nor in the past,
And did yourself no good, when in despite of friends
You gave your favour to your furious heart, which has
Undone you always.[84]

CHORUS

Hold there, stranger!

CREON

Touch me not, I tell you!

CHORUS

I will not let you go, and be defrauded of these children.

CREON

Then you will quickly raise the stakes
Of the city's quarrel: for I will seize
Not just two girls.   990

CHORUS

What will you turn to now?

CREON

I will lead that man away, captive.

CHORUS

You speak fiercely.

CREON

It will be done, even now.

CHORUS

Not if the ruler of this ground prevents it.

OEDIPUS

O shameless voice! Will you light upon me still?

CREON

Speak silently.

OEDIPUS

The Goddesses have not yet made me mute
For this my curse and prayer: thou most evil man,

That would force from me, who have no eyes,   1000
My helpless one, who was my eyes till now.
Therefore to thee and thy family may the God
All-seeing-Helios grant an old age just like mine.

CREON

Do you see these things, men of this country?

OEDIPUS

Let them see you and me, and think
That having suffered in deeds,
I requited you with words.

CREON

I will not check my rage: I shall lead this man away,
Though all alone, and slow with age.

OEDIPUS

O, sorry man!   1010

CHORUS

In such audacity you come here, stranger,
If you think to finish your attempt!

CREON

I do.

CHORUS

Then I shall consider Athens a city no longer.

CREON

In a just cause, a feeble man might overcome
Great opposition.

OEDIPUS

Do you hear his mutterings?

CHORUS

But they will not be fulfilled:
Zeus knows this with me.

CREON

Zeus might know, but you do not.   1020

CHORUS

Is this not hubris?

CREON

Hubris, yes; but reality as well.

CHORUS

O all the people, O foremost of men,

Hither come quickly, come!
For they approach indeed our very borders —

Enter THESEUS

THESEUS
Why this shout? What's the matter?
In what fear have you halted
My sacrifice of bulls upon the altar
Of the Ocean God, that in Colonus stands?
Tell me, so that I may know all,   1030
For which I hurried here more in haste
Than in the pleasure of my feet.

OEDIPUS
O dearest man, I recognise your voice!
I have suffered, grievously, and by this very man!

THESEUS
You suffered what? What was the injury?
Tell.

OEDIPUS
This Creon, the man you have seen,
Left here, having torn from me my only children.

THESEUS
How claim you this?

OEDIPUS
I have suffered it, just as you heard it.   1040

THESEUS
Let someone of my servants, fast as possible, go:
Have all the people hasten from the sacrifice;
Those without horses, and the mounted ones,
With their reins let loose;[85] and in the region
Where the two roads meet, converge
Upon the travellers: lest the daughters cross,
And I become a jest for this foreign man,
As though he handled me with force. Go,
As I commanded; with speed! [*turning to Creon*] And this one,
If I were as angry as he deserves,   1050
I would not loose him from my grip
Uninjured. Now, by that selfsame law
He came here intending to enforce

He himself shall be arrested; none beside.
You will never leave this land, until
You lead those girls to stand here manifest
Before me. What you have done is disgraceful
To me, to those from whom you were born,
And to your homeland. You have entered a city
That thinks on justice, not without fulfilment   1060
Of the law: what though you dismiss this sovereign place
Of Earth; though you traduce us here, ·
And lead off whom you will, and use compulsion,
Thinking my city to be empty of men, or like
Some city of slaves, and I like some nonentity.
Yet surely Thebes did not teach you evil.
For they love not men in whom injustice springs,
Nor would they approve, if they learned
That you seize what belongs to me and to the Gods,
Leading off helpless suppliant men by force.   1070
If I had entered upon your land, never, not even
Were I charged with all the most just cause,
Without permission of whoever was the sovereign
Would I lead nor arrest any in the land; but I would know
How a guest in a city must conduct himself.
You disgrace a city that deserves no such disgrace:
Your own city; you disgrace your advancing age
Which finds you empty-minded as you are.
I have told you already, and I repeat it now:
With all speed let the children be brought here,   1080
Unless you intend to remain abroad for a spell,
Compelled, against your will. These things
I tell you with my tongue just as in my mind
I think them.

CHORUS

Do you see what you have come to, stranger?
As for whom you come from, they seem just:
But they find your actions evil.

CREON

I do not hold this city to be void of men,
O child of Aegeus, nor void of counsel, as you said.
This deed I performed in the certain knowledge   1090

That your people would not be so eager for my own
Blood kinsmen, as forcefully to keep them from me.
You would not do this, I was sure, for a man
Who had killed his father. You would not receive
One who was utterly unclean, a man who,
With his unholy bride, had been found out
In the vile marriage of a parent to her child.
Such is the wisdom of them, established
In the Court of Ares, native to this country;[86]
I was sure of it: that institution would not suffer   1100
Such a vagrant as this man to dwell inside the city:
So in that belief, I took it in hand to catch him.
And I had not done so, had he not denounced me[87]
And my family with that stabbing curse: suffering which,
This seemed a just thing to inflict in turn.
Anger cannot age away; it dies only
At utter death. And no pain touches the dead.[88]
Toward these things, respond as you like.
Though I am alone, and though that make me slight,
Yet I speak like a just man. Though I am old,   1110
I will endeavour to respond in kind, deed for deed.

OEDIPUS

O shameless arrogance! Is it my own old age,
Or yours, that you would heap with this abuse?
What murder and marriage and event
You spit from your mouth for my reproach,
That I performed but wretchedly, unwilling,
Not choosing? It was dear to the Gods that way.[89]
Maybe They were angry with my family, from the past,
Since for my part, you could not find in me
The guilt of any sin, that these (my crimes   1120
Against myself and mine) might answer for.
Otherwise, teach me:[90] if by some oracle
Come unto him, my father was condemned
So that he die by his own child, how then
Can you reproach me justly for it?
No father had as yet engendered me;
I had no mother, but was unborn as ever.
And if, appearing on the scene, I was a wretch

(As I was shown to be[91]), and came to blows
With my father and killed him, not understanding   1130
What I was doing nor to whom I was doing it,
How can you blame an unwilled deed, and be just?
And my mother! Thou sorry knave, that feel no shame
At forcing me to speak of her marriage of incest
When she was thy sister, such things as I speak now.
I will not be silent then, since in your mouth's impiety
You do exceed. For she gave birth to me; oh, misery!
She was my mother, though I knew it not, and she
Knew it neither. She brought me into the world,
And to her infamy she bore me children.   1140
But one thing I know full well: me and her
You willingly denounce with these affairs,
So I married unknowingly, and now unwilling
I declare these things. But I will not hear myself
Denounced as evil for this marriage, nor for that
Murder of my father which you goad me with forever.
Now answer me one question I will ask you.
If someone making you stand aside, here and now,
Should try to kill you, would you learn by asking him
If the killer were your father, or would you deal with him,   1150
Straight away? It seems to me, if you like to live,
You would repay the man responsible,
And not go searching for the right.
Into such a sort of evils I myself stepped,
Led on by the Gods. In this I do not think
My father's soul, if he lived, would contradict me.
But you, since you are not a just man,
But consider anything appropriate to say,
With such words, both spoken and implied
Before these men you have denounced me.   1160
It seems expedient to you to flatter Theseus'
Noble name, and Athens' fine administration.
And yet, as you say so much, something escapes you:
That if any land knows how to worship the Gods aright,
This one excels in it, out from which to steal me,
A suppliant old man, you came here.
You tried for me with your hands, and my daughters

You have taken away.[92] For this, I now supplicate
These Goddesses, now implore Them with my prayers;
I come calling on Them, to come to me   1170
As my rescuing allies, that you may learn
What sort of men they are who keep the watch
About this city.

CHORUS

This stranger, O my King, is earnest,
Though his circumstance was all-destroying
And deserves our sympathy.

THESEUS

Plenty of talk, while the guilty men speed
And we who suffer stand about.

CREON

What would you command your helpless man
To do?   1180

THESEUS

That you lead us in their path, and I go with you,
So that if you hold these children within my realm,
You will present them for me; but if your men escape
With them in tow, then there is nothing we need do.
For others speed the chase, because of whom your men
Shall never thank the Gods for their escape from here.
Now lead the way: and know, the taker is taken;
And fate has taken you, though you were hunting.
For the gains of wrongful provocation none may keep.
And you will have no partner in this enterprise: 1190
For I know well, that you were not alone, nor unprepared,
When you offered your outrageous show of violence
Just now, but as you did this you were trusting in another.
And I must look to these things, lest this my city
Be made weaker than a single man. Heed you this,
Or do these things I have said seem vain to you
As did those warnings when you planned your deeds?

CREON

Say to me what you will, without reproach,
While we are here: but when we have come home,
We too shall know what we must do.   1200

THESEUS

Threaten if you will, only go now: but you,
Oedipus, so please you, stay here in peace,
Trusting that unless I die first, I shall never stop
Until I put thee back in charge of thy children.

OEDIPUS

Bless you, Theseus, for your grace to me,
And for the justice of your noble foresight.

[*Exeunt Creon and Theseus*

Fourth Choral Ode[93]

CHORUS

Would that I were present where the enemy men
Will plunge and speeding turn in the bronze war-noise
Of Ares, near the torch-lit, or near the Pythian shores,
Where the holy Goddesses tend the dead with rites,   1210
Upon whose lips the ministrant Eumolpidae have laid
The golden seal: there, I think, the battle-rousing Theseus
Will meet with those journeying sisters twain,
And meet their guards, amid a war cry of his own.

Or perhaps the quarry will approach
The region westward of the snowy rock,
When they have left the Oeatid country,
Racing away on young horses, or in chariots
Careening. There shall be an overtaking.
The war strength of the natives there is terrible,   1220
And terrible is the power of Theseus' young soldiers.
Each bridle flashes lightning, and with every rein let loose,
All the horsemen speed away, that worship
Athena of the Horses, and the world-embracing
Ancient of the sea, the dear son of Rhea.

Is the fight on now, or yet to come?
My thought suggests that soon they will return them,
The girls in their terrible ordeal, who first were found
By suffering at a kinsman's hands. Today, today, Zeus,
Bring to pass what we desire! I am a prophet   1230
In predicting our good ending for the struggle!
If only I could light upon their fighting from above them,

Like a strong-winged dove through the storming upper air,
Gazing with my eyes from far above them!

O Zeus, who rule all heaven and see all,
Grant that this land's guardians fill with strength
For victory-crowned success in the ambush;
And so grant Thy holy child, Pallas Athena.
And Apollo the Hunter, and His sister,
That follows the spotted and swift-footed deer: 1240
I want Them to come to this country, and to these citizens,
A pair of defenders.
O foreign wanderer, you will not call my divination false:
I can see the two girls coming near, with attendants
Just behind them.

Enter THESEUS, ANTIGONE *and* ISMENE

OEDIPUS

Where, where? What have you said?
What are you saying?

ANTIGONE

O, Father! Father! Which of the Gods
Might grant you to see this greatest of men,
Who has brought us here before you?   1250

OEDIPUS

O my child, are you here?

ANTIGONE

Here we are, for the arms of Theseus
And his most dear followers have saved us.

OEDIPUS

Come here, my child, to your father,
Give me to embrace you, who beyond hope
Have returned!

ANTIGONE

What you have asked for, receive;
For we have yearned to give it.

OEDIPUS

Where then, where are you?

ANTIGONE

We both are near you.   1260

OEDIPUS

O, my dearest issue!

ANTIGONE

Dear to the one who brought us into life.

OEDIPUS

O crutches for a man!

ANTIGONE

With our sad share of your portion's sorrow.

OEDIPUS

I hold my dearest ones, and were I to die now,
With these two here beside me, yet I would not grieve.
Support me on both sides, my children,
Cling to me; and lean upon your father;
Rest from this late desolate and bitter wandering.
And tell me what happened, briefly as you can,   1270
Since at your age a short speech is enough.

ANTIGONE

This is our saviour: you must hear it from him,
Because the deed was his. And thus so brief
Shall be my portion.

OEDIPUS

O my host, do not marvel, if persisting I prolong
My conversation with my children late-appearing,
Past my hopes. For I well know that this my joy in them
Proceeds from you, for you have saved them,
And no other mortal man. And may the Gods treat you
As I have wished, you and this your country: 1280
For among you alone of mankind have I found
Equity, noble piety, and the refusal to speak lies.
I know these things whereof I speak, and I repay them:
For what I have, I have through you,
And through no other mortal. Reach out to me
Your right hand, O King, that I may touch it,
And if custom permits, that I may kiss your head.
And yet, what have I said? How could I wish
You to touch a man who has become the host
For every stain of evil? I would not let you,   1290
Not even were you willing. Among mortals
Only those can share this suffering who have it

By experience. Receive you then my thanks
From where you are; care for me in justice
For my remaining days, as you have this day.

THESEUS

I do not marvel at it, if you speak at length
At the return of these your delightful children,
Nor marvel if you listen to their words before my own.
Nothing heavy in that for us. For we are eager
That we must make our life to shine; and not by words,   1300
Rather by the things we do. And this I demonstrate.
For in that oath which I did swear to you, old man,
I did not lie. For here I am, leading them alive,
Unscathed by the vaunted threats. As for how
This fight was thus achieved, it were vain indeed
To boast the tale you soon shall hear from these
Your two companions. But on my way here,
A certain argument occurred to me, to which
I should like you to contribute your opinion,
For though it be spoken briefly, yet it is worthy   1310
Of some wonder, and what is compelling
One must not dismiss.

OEDIPUS

What is it, child of Aegeus? Teach me,
And we will see whether I am not ignorant
Upon the subject you address.

THESEUS

It is said that some man, not your countryman
But a relative of yours, has somehow
Thrown himself upon Poseidon's altar
For asylum, at which I had been sacrificing
When I set out here.   1320

OEDIPUS

From what land is he? What does he need
By his sitting there?

THESEUS

I know only this, that it is your audience
He comes to beg, for a brief speech,
Of no great moment.[94]

OEDIPUS

Of what sort? That seat is no place
For trivial words.

THESEUS

They say he asks only to come and speak with you,
And to be secure in his road away from here.

OEDIPUS   1330

Who indeed is this, that takes the holy seat?

THESEUS

See whether you have any kinsman of Argos,
Who might want something of you?

OEDIPUS

O dear man, hold, whatever else it is!

THESEUS

What is that to you?

OEDIPUS

Don't ask me!

THESEUS

About what? Tell me.

OEDIPUS

Hearing what you say, I know who has come
For sanctuary.

THESEUS

And who is this man, that I should quarrel with him?

OEDIPUS

My child, O King, my hated child, whose words   1340
Of all mankind's I would most bitterly resist the hearing.

THESEUS

Why? To listen is not to do the things
You would not be compelled to do.
Why should it hurt you to hear them?

OEDIPUS

O my King, that voice of his has become
To his father most hateful. Do not force me
To yield in this.

THESEUS

But consider if his supplication compels you,
Must you not attend to what concerns the Gods?

ANTIGONE

   Father, heed me, and though I am young,   1350
   I will advise you. Allow this man
   The grace of what is in his heart,
   And gratify the Gods as he wishes.
   Yield to us, and let our brother come.
   For take courage, he cannot change your mind
   By force, unless the things he tells you matter.
   What harm is it to hear a speech?
   The deeds we do in evil are stripped bare
   Through speaking. You begat him:
   Therefore, not even if he did you the most impious   1360
   Of wicked wrongs, my father, were it pious
   To requite him in kind. No, allow him:
   There are other men who have bad children,
   And sharp tempers, but they have this ill nature
   Charmed out of them by the spell of their dear ones.
   Look you now, not into the present, but the past,
   And all that at your mother's and your father's hands
   You suffered: if you look there closely, I am sure,
   You will know what evil follows from evil anger.
   You have plenty of examples on which to think;   1370
   Your own blindness, your want of eyes. But yield to us:
   It is not noble to refuse a just entreaty,
   Nor that a man should benefit from kindness
   And then not know how to be kind in turn.

OEDIPUS

   O child, with the pleasure of your reasoning
   I am won over, though it be heavy.
   But let this be, as it is dear to you.
   But if indeed that man is to come here, sir,
   I only ask that no man ever rule my life with force.

THESEUS

   One need hear such a thing but once, old man,   1380
   Not twice. And I have no wish to boast. But know
   You are safe, so long as any of the Gods preserves me.

                                      [Exit Theseus

Fifth Choral Ode

CHORUS

Whoever craves a greater portion of longevity,
And does not want the modest share — in my view,
Such a man is bound to foolishness. For the long days
Heap up a shambles, closer to grief and pain,
Whereas he will no more know his pleasures,
Or their place, when into life's excess he has declined.
But the soothing death ends all alike,
With their portion in Hades, that suddenly appears   1390
Without the lyre, the marriage song, the chorus:
Death at last.

Not to be born, surpasses all argument:
But once a man is born, the second best
Is his swift return whence he came.
When youth, with its levity and unwisdom
Has passed him by, what grievous stroke
Remains outside his life? What toil is not inside it?
Destruction, quarrels, fighting, battles,
Even murders. Last, loveless old age   1400
Is his lot next; blamed, rejected,
Powerless old age, and with him
The worst of all evils dwell together.

Such a man endures this plight, long-suffering:
(It is not only I who so endure) and like some northern coast
Lashed by the driven billows of the winter storm,
Even thus the man is inundated utterly
By ever-present terrors that upon him break like waves:
Those from the direction of the setting of the sun,
Those from the sun's rising,   1410
Those from the southerly noonday sun,
And those from northern mountains in the night.

ANTIGONE

Lo, there, coming toward us is the visitor, I think,
With no henchmen, my father; and as he walks the road,
Tears stream from his eyes.

Enter POLYNEICES

OEDIPUS
    Who is it then?
ANTIGONE
    The very man we held in our thoughts before:
    This is Polyneices, present here.
POLYNEICES
    Oh me, what am I to do? Shall I weep for my past evils,
    Sisters, or for those of my old father, whom I see before me?   1420
    Whom I have found on foreign soil, in exile with the
                                                two of you;
    The ill–loved old man in his robes, whereon the old dirt
                                                dwells still,
    Wasting his ribs away; and on his eyeless head
    The uncombed white shocks quiver on the breeze.
    The diet of his wretched stomach is, in him,
    A brother to these traits. See what a wretch I am,
    That learn this too late; and let me bear witness
    That I have become the vilest of men, in this neglect
    Of your sustenance. Take this from my own lips,
    Not from others'. But since Zeus himself in all affairs   1430
    Has Mercy as the sharer of His throne, closer to thee,
    Father, may that spirit draw. For there is yet
    A remedy for your mistakes, whereas they cannot
    Be made worse. Why are you silent? Tell me,
    Father, why? Do not turn away from me.
    Will you answer me nothing, but in contempt
    Will you send me off without hearing your voice?
    Nor tell me what angers you? You then, seed of this man,
    And sisters of my blood, try and move our implacable father,
    Whom one can hardly confront with the words of one's mouth,   1440
    Lest he dishonour me, who am a suppliant of the God,
    And dismiss me thus, without a word in answer.
ANTIGONE
    Tell him yourself, unhappy man, what you require now.
    For a plea of many words can waken joy, or consternation,
    Or deep pity, so that silent people speak.
POLYNEICES
    I shall tell him all then (for you counsel me nobly),
    First making propitious the God from whose altar

The king of this land has raised me up, to come here;
And has given me leave to speak, and to hear, and to return
Unharmed. And these pledgèd things I shall want from you,   1450
My hosts, and from my sisters and my father,
That I should have them. But now I want to tell you
What I came for, O my father. Out into exile
I have been driven from my fatherland,
Because I thought me worthy, being eldest born,
To seat me in your absolute and ancient throne.
In recompense, Eteocles, who was the younger born,
Expelled me from the country, though he prevailed
Neither in discourse, nor in cross examination,
Nor in deeds of hands: He came and won the city over.   1460
Of this, I think, the cause lies in your Furies;[95]
And I hear the like from soothsayers.
So then I came to Doric Argos, where Adrastus
Became my father-in-law. The dwellers in Apian land[96]
Are foremost in the honour and fame of their spears:
I had them pledge me their allegiance in an oath,
That marshalling their seven spear divisions,
I might Thebes attempt, either to die in my all-righteous cause,
Or banish from the land the men responsible.
Well then: why do I come here now?   1470
To turn to you with prayers, O my father, my own prayers
And those of my allies, who now with seven spears
Lead seven armies to their stations, filling all the plain
Of Thebes. Such is spear-throwing Amphiaraus,
First in the strength of his spear and first alike in augury.
The second is Tydeus, the son of Aetolian Oineus.
Eteoclus is third, born in Argos. Fourth, Hippomedon
Sent by his father Talaos. The fifth one, Capaneus,
Boasts that he will burn Thebes down with fire,
To the ground. Sixth, Parthenopaeus is roused from Arcadia   1480
For the war, named for his mother who had long been a virgin;
He is Atalanta's faithful son.[97] I am your son,
And if I am not yours, but am planted by some evil fate,
Yet I am called your son, and I lead the fearless Argives
Against the Theban army. All we men entreat you
By these children, father, by your own life, we beseech you,

Give me up your heavy anger as I move against my brother,
That thrust me from my country, and hath stolen it.
For if our faith repose in oracles, they say that power
Shall be with that side you espouse, my father.   1490
And now I ask you, by the sacred rivers and Gods
Of our familial nation, to yield and be persuaded,
Since we are beggars and exiles, as you are an exile.
You and I make our homes by flattering other men;
The spirit of our fortunes is the same. But he
That is the tyrant in our halls, while I am wretched,
Mocks at us both alike in laughter: whom,
If you will take my cause to heart, I shall
Without much time or trouble, scatter to the winds.
Leading you back thus, I shall establish you again   1500
In your own halls, and myself establish, when with violence
I have thrown him out. If you will want these things with me,
Then I may boast that my own strength will save me not
Without your own.

CHORUS
For the sake of him who sent this man,[98] Oedipus,
Tell him what you would, and send him back again.

OEDIPUS
Well then, you men of this land that tends the people,
Had Theseus himself not sent this man to me here,
It would not be just to hear from me these words,
Nor ever know my solemn voice herein. But as it is,   1510
He finds him worthy such things to hear from me
As never shall make glad his life. O worst of men,
Who, when you held the sceptre and the throne,
Which now in Thebes your brother holds,
You drove me out, who am your own father;
Made me a stateless refugee; made me to carry
Such equipment as you now have wept to look upon,
Now that you also happen upon laborious sorrows
Like my own. It is not to be wept over;
I am to endure this while I live, and think of you   1520
As of a murderer. For it was you that set me up so,
Turning me thus to hardship and drudgery;
You that forced me out; from you proceeds my life

Of vagrancy, my begging others for my sustenance.
As for your part, if I had not had these my daughters,
I would be no more; they preserve me even now;
They are my caretakers; in their work together
These girls are men, not women. But you were born
From others, not from me. Therefore indeed
The daimon looks on you, not yet as it soon shall,   If indeed 1530
those armies move upon the Theban town,[99]
Since you can never bring that city down to ruin,
But before then you will fall, polluted
With a brother's blood, and he polluted
With your own alike. These are the sort of curses
I called down ere now upon you both;
Curses I now call upon to come to me, as allies,
That you may think it right to hold your parents
In some reverence, and not be scornful utterly,
Because your father is blind who made sons like you.   1540
For these two girls do not act as you have acted.
My curses rule your pleading, and this throne of yours,
If the ancient law pronounced so long ago still holds,
That at the throne of Zeus is Justice also seated.
But you, go: I spit out and despise you
As the worst of wicked men; you have no father in me.
Take together these curses I call down on you,
That neither shall you overcome with spears
The city of your kin, nor return to Argos valley, ever:
But with a brother's hand, and by a brother's hand,   1550
Shall you murder and be killed by him that banished you.
For such things I have prayed; and I call upon Tartarus'
Stygian darkness, paternal,[100] that it bring you out from home;
I call upon these Goddesses, and on Ares yet I call,
Who has cast into you both his terrible hatred.
Go on, with these things in your ears, and announce
To all the people of Thebes and to those allies
To whom you plight your faith, that Oedipus
Has divided thus the inheritance of his sons.

CHORUS

Polyneices, I take no pleasure in your journeys past;   1560
Now get you home again in speed.

POLYNEICES

Alas, for my journey and my failure! Alas,
For my companions!
What an ending of my road
From Argos! What a miserable man I am!
I cannot speak such things to my companions,
Nor turn them back again, but I must silently
Confront the outcome! But O you his daughters
And sisters mine, since you heard yourselves
Our father speak his dire sentence, you at least,   1570
If his curses find fulfilment from the Gods,
And somehow you should find a way back home
To Thebes, do not dishonour me, but place me in a tomb
With funeral gifts. The praise you earn from this man now
Shall yet increase with other praise, because you do this labour
For me.

ANTIGONE

Polyneices, I beg you, in one thing,
Be persuaded by me!

POLYNEICES

O dearest Antigone, what sort of thing?
Tell me.

ANTIGONE As soon as possible to turn your army back to Argos,   1580
Lest you destroy yourself and Thebes our city.

POLYNEICES

But I cannot. For how could I possibly lead an army
A second time, once I had retreated with it?

ANTIGONE

Still, why need your anger come again, child?
What profits you your fatherland's destruction?

POLYNEICES

It is shameful to flee, when I am the elder,
And shameful to be mocked thus by my brother.

ANTIGONE [indicating Oedipus]

Do you see his predictions coming strictly true,
Who cries aloud that both you brothers will destroy
Each other?   1590

POLYNEICES

Yes, for he wishes it. But I must not give in.[101]

ANTIGONE [*indicating Oedipus*]

 O me, wretched! And what man will dare to follow you,
 Hearing what this man hath prophesied?

POLYNEICES

 I shall not announce his mutterings: for an effective general
 Tells the greater strength, and does not tell the desperation.

ANTIGONE

 It seems that way to you, does it, child?

POLYNEICES

 And do not keep me. For this is my ill-fated road,
 Whereon I have to go, and with me, evil from my father
 And his Furies. But you, may Zeus be good to you,
 If you do these things for me when I am dead,   1600
 Since while I live there is no more for you to do.
 Let me go. I must bid you farewell now.
 You will never see me alive again.[102]

ANTIGONE

 Oh, I am miserable!

POLYNEICES

 Do not lament me.

ANTIGONE

 And who would not lament a brother
 That enters on a death foreknown?

POLYNEICES

 If necessary, I will die.

ANTIGONE

 Do not die, but heed me then!

POLYNEICES

 Do not argue for what must not be.   1610

ANTIGONE

 Bereaved of you, I shall be wretched!

POLYNEICES

 It rests with the divine to bring that forth,
 Or something else. As for the two of you,
 I pray that you never meet with evils,
 For in all men's sight, you deserve not oppression.

            [*Exit Polyneices*

[*intermittent thunder*]

CHORUS

From new events, new evils of heavy misfortune
Come into my ken, from our blind guest, unless
Some fate is reaching to its issue. For it is not mine
To call divine decisions vain. Time watches and watches
Such decisions ever, running some men down,   1620
And on the morrow, lifting others up again.
O Zeus! The thunder crashes in the upper air!

OEDIPUS

O children, children, I need someone to go
And bring the best of all men, Theseus.

ANTIGONE

Father, what is this for which you call on him?

OEDIPUS

This winged thunder of Zeus will lead me to Hades soon;
Send for him, as quickly as you can.
[thunder]

CHORUS

Behold the great unspeakable noise of thunder crashing down,
Thrown by Zeus; the terror of it makes my hair to stand on end;
Fear mounts up to my head; my heart is cowering.   1630
Again, the lightning flashes in the heavens.
What event can this portend? I do fear it:
For this stirs never in vain, never without a consequence.[103]
O great sky! O Zeus!

OEDIPUS

My children, the ending of my life which God predicted
Comes upon me, and there can be no refusal.

ANTIGONE

How do you know? What brought the notion to you?

OEDIPUS

I know it well. But swift as may be, let someone go
And bring the monarch of this country to my side.

CHORUS

Oh, oh! Mark again that piercing, all-surrounding sound!   1640
Be merciful, merciful, O Divinities, if at all
You harbour dark intentions for our mother earth.
Let me find favour with you; and do not,

Because I have beheld a cursed man,
Make me to share some portion to my detriment;
Zeus above me, to Thee I speak.

OEDIPUS

But is the man nearby? Will he find me alive yet,
Children, and in my right mind still?

ANTIGONE

What pledge is it you would plant in his heart?

OEDIPUS

In exchange for my good welfare, I promised him   1650
I would give him grace when I had gained my request.

CHORUS

Oh, oh! Child, come here, come! If at the furthest reaches
Of the hollow in the wooded glen, with the sacrifice you feast
The Sea God Poseidon; come!
You and your city and your friends
The stranger finds worthy of a just thanks
For being treated justly. Come, O King!

Enter THESEUS

THESEUS

What great thunder is this, that pours from you again,
Clearly from the town, manifestly from our foreigner?
Unless that was some thunderbolt of Zeus, or else some rain   1660
Or dashing hail? One may expect anything
When such a storm as this comes from the God.

OEDIPUS

O King, they long for your presence, and some God
Has blessed your noble fortune with your road here.

THESEUS

What news, child of Laius?

OEDIPUS

My life's end. And those things I agreed upon
With you, about the city – I do not wish to die a liar.

THESEUS

What sign of your fate do you repose upon?

OEDIPUS

What the Gods themselves as messengers announced to me
And what they long ago established does not lie.   1670

THESEUS

How do you say the Gods have shown these things?

OEDIPUS

Those many and ongoing thunders and flashes
Of lightning thrown from the unconquered hand.

THESEUS

I am persuaded. For I see you prophesying many things
And none of them is false. Say then, what must be done.

OEDIPUS

I shall teach you, child of Aegeus, something your city
Shall lay up in store, for a painless old age. Soon,
I shall lead the way to the very spot: I shall be the leader,
Untouched, toward the place where I must die.
But never reveal this to another human soul,   1680
Neither where it is hidden, nor the region where it lies:
Thus for you it shall be set there as a strength
Greater than your many shields and the spears of your allies.
But those things of which it is a curse to set a word in motion,
You shall learn them yourself, then, when you come there alone,
Since I can reveal them neither to the people of this town
Nor to my children, though I love them. But keep it
Always to yourself, and when you come into the end of life,
Reveal it only to your sole favourite; and he to his successor,
Forever. Thus shall you dwell in this city unmolested   1690
By men from the Theban side; but many cities,
Though well governed, come to aggression lightly.
For the Gods look well, though slowly, when one turns
From godly things to mad ambition. This you must not
Be willing to suffer, child of Aegeus. But here
I am teaching these things to one who knows them.
Nay but the spot the God revealed compels me;
Let us hurry now, nor yet be turned from the way.
My children, follow, this way. For I have been made
Your guide again, just as you guided your father.   1700
Come away, and touch me not, but allow me
By myself to discover my sacred tomb, in that place
Where it is this man's portion to be hidden in the ground.
This is the way; this way, step this way. For they lead me on,
Hermes the Guide, and the netherworldly Goddess. O Light,

That now is no light, I suppose I had you once. I feel you now
Upon my frame, the final time. For I already crawl
Toward the ending of my life, concealed in Hades.
But you, O dearest of hosts or guests, you and your land
And your people, may your happiness thrive,   1710
And in your good fortune, remember me that died;
Farewell, forever.   [*Oedipus passes from the stage,*
                                followed by all but the Chorus

CHORUS

If it is permitted me to worship You with prayers,
Goddess Invisible, and You, Lord of Darkness, Hades,
Hades, I pray to you, that with no painful labour,
Nor heavy grief, in accord with fate, our guest
May reach the all-concealing field,
Of the dead, and the Stygian House.
For his many and fruitless sufferings
The justice of the Gods will yet exalt him.   1720

O Earthly Goddesses, and the unvanquished beast of flesh[104]
That lie in ambush for so many guests between those doors,
And growl from the caves, unconquered guardian of Hades,
As has been legend always, I pray to you,
O child of Earth and Tartarus, step clear of this stranger
As he moves upon the plains of the dead, the netherworld.
I call upon you, that you may hear me, giver of eternal sleep.

                    Enter a MESSENGER

MESSENGER

Citizen men, my news most briefly: Oedipus has perished.
But one cannot tell so briefly what transpired there,
Nor were the actions of it brief.   1730
CHORUS

The poor man is dead, then?
MESSENGER

That man, be sure of it, has left this life.
CHORUS

How? Did the Goddess send him a painless death?
MESSENGER

Now comes the point that is worthy of amazement.

How he crept from here, you surely know,
As you were present. He had no guide among his friends,
But he himself led all of us on: when he arrived
Upon that road that rushes downward,
The brazen stairway rooted in the Earth,[105]
He stood upon one trail among the many branching paths   1740
Near to that hollow bowl of stone where Theseus
And Peirithous laid down eternal pledges of their faith:
Midway between this and the Thorician rock he stood,[106]
And sat him down between a stone tomb and the hollow tree,
Of wild pear; and there he loosed his filthy clothes,
And calling on his children bid them bring
From the river water for his bath, and his libations.
They came to Demeter's conspicuous, verdant hill
And in a little while, brought quickly what their father wanted;
Then with robes and cleansing they accoutred him   1750
As custom bids. But when he had his satisfaction
With their every labour, and nothing lay neglected
Nor remained undone, the Zeus of the Ground
Crashed, and the virgins shuddered hearing it;
They fell weeping to their father's knees, nor ceased
To beat their breasts, while in their keening they continued long.
But when he heard their sudden bitter cry,
He put his arms about them, saying: 'Children,
No longer from today have you a father. For now,
Everything has perished that was mine; and no longer   1760
Shall you bear the heavy burden of my care.
I know it was hard, my children; yet one word
Dissolves those hardships all: the love you had from me
No other has exceeded, and you now
Must live the rest of your lives through without me.'
They all embraced each other at these words,
And cried out sobbing. But when they came
Toward the end of their lamenting, and no more
Stirred their shouts, there was a silence, and then
A voice, suddenly speaking to him, so that suddenly   1770
All the hair of their heads stood up for fear. For the God
Many times in many tones upon him called, 'O Oedipus,
Why do we delay our journey? You have tarried so.'

When he heard himself thus called on by the God,
He asked that Theseus, the king of this land, come to him.
And when he came, he said to him: O dear one,
Give me your hand, and your oath of faith to my children,
And you, daughters, to him. Promise you will never
Willingly betray them, but always in kind intention   1780
Look after them.' And without lamenting, he like a noble man
Assented to this oath, to do what he promised him.
When he had done these things, Oedipus
Feeling with his blind hands for his children, told them:
'O children, you must do the noble deed you have in mind
And leave this place: do not ask to see what you should not,
Nor hear the speaking voices you should not. Go quickly:
Let only Theseus be present, whose right it is, to learn
What will be done.' So much we all heard him say,
And grieving aloud we followed the girls.   1790
But when we had moved on, after a moment we turned
And behold, the man was nowhere present anymore;
But the king alone, holding his hand against his face
To spare his eyes the terror of some apparition marvellous
That none can bear to see. Then a moment later on,
We saw him make obeisance to the Earth,
And in the same prayers, to Olympus of the Gods.
But by what kind of fate that man died, there is no one
Among mortals who can tell, except for Theseus.
For he was not destroyed by any fire-bearing stroke
Of lightning from the God, nor by some whirlwind   1800
Landward sweeping at that moment from the sea: but either
Someone of the Gods was his leader hence, or else
The kindly Earth gaped open for him, to the painless
Firm foundation of the netherworld. For the man
Made no groans; nor did he depart with pains of sickness,
But if any mortal's death be something marvellous,
This was. And if I do not seem to speak wisely,
I do not address those to whom I seem unwise.

CHORUS
    And where are those two girls, and those of our friends
    Sent with them?   1810

MESSENGER

They are not far. For their voices, not without weeping
Tell that they move hereabout.

Enter ANTIGONE *and* ISMENE

ANTIGONE

Aiai, pheu! Now indeed it is ours to cry out lamentation
Utterly, on our father's cursed blood, born in us to our undoing
Although until now we did much ongoing labour for this man,
Yet in the end we shall bring from it the having suffered and seen
What lies the furthest from speech and reason.

CHORUS

What is it?

ANTIGONE

We may conjecture, O friends.

CHORUS

Is he gone?[107]

1820

ANTIGONE

Yes, and yet you might long for it to come this way;
For neither by Ares nor by the Ocean was he covered over,
Random things; but the very fields have seized him,
Carried him off in some invisible fate. We are wretched,
And a night of destruction has come upon our eyes.
For how shall we gain our living, wandering
In some distant country's hardship, or on the sea waves?

ISMENE

I know not. I wish murderous Hades would take me down
To die with our old father. Wretched, how the life I will lead
Seems lifeless to me.

1830

CHORUS

You two daughters most noble, bear what burden
You must carry from the God, and do not burn with grief's
                                                excess.
You have come to fair results.

ANTIGONE

Then there is such a thing as longing for troubles.
For indeed things are dear to me, that were not dear at all
Then, when I held him in my hands.

O father, O dear one, O man wrapped in the eternal dark 1700
Beneath the earth: down below you shall not be unloved,
By me, nor by her.

CHORUS

How fared he?   1840

ANTIGONE

He fared but as he would.

CHORUS

How so?

ANTIGONE

In that he died upon the foreign soil he had chosen;
But now he has the sweet shade of his bed below forever,
Nor did he leave behind a mourning without tears.
O father, with tearful eyes I cry out for you;
So much is my wretched grief in loss of you,
I cannot make it disappear. Oh me!
You chose to die upon a foreign spot of earth,
But now you have died alone, without me.[108]   1850

ISMENE

Unhappy one, what fate awaits you and me,
That have no father now?

CHORUS

But since he has reached the end of his life in blessedness,
Dear girls, leave your lamentation. Evils are not to be outstripped.

ANTIGONE

Sister, let us hurry back again.

ISMENE

What shall we accomplish thus?

ANTIGONE

A longing takes me.

ISMENE

What is it?

ANTIGONE

To look upon his dwelling in the ground.

ISMENE

Whose?   1860

ANTIGONE

Our father's, wretch that I am!

ISMENE

But how can this be proper?
That it is not, surely you can see.

ANTIGONE

What is this insult?

ISMENE

And this, too –

ANTIGONE

What is this else?

ISMENE

That he fell without a tomb, apart from all.

ANTIGONE

Lead me there, and kill me.

ISMENE

Aiai. Poor wretch, how am I to sustain
My sorry life, alone, with no way forward?   1870

CHORUS

Friends, do not flee in fear.

ISMENE

But to where can I escape?

CHORUS

You have already escaped from evils.

ANTIGONE

How?

CHORUS

By our provision that your fortunes not fall ill.

ANTIGONE

I know it well.

CHORUS

Then what do you think on?

ANTIGONE

I know not how we might return
To our own home.

CHORUS

You must not seek to do so.   1880

ANTIGONE

Trouble besets us.

CHORUS
And it has done so before.
ANTIGONE
Hopeless then, and now worse yet.
CHORUS
Great indeed is the sea of grief you twain
Have for your lot in life.
ANTIGONE
Pheu, Pheu! O Zeus, where shall we go?
What hope remains to us, driven on our course by fate?

THESEUS
Stop lamenting, children. For when the favour of the powers
                                                     below
Is laid in store as a benefit in common, one must not lament.
It would bring Nemesis.[109]   1890
ANTIGONE
O child of Aegeus, we supplicate you!
THESEUS
To fill what need of yours, children?
ANTIGONE
We two wish to see the tomb of our father.
THESEUS
But this is not pious.
ANTIGONE
How can you say that, Lord of Athens?
THESEUS
O children, to me that man forbade
That any should approach the place;
Forbade that any mortal voice should speak
Over the holy grave that is his own.
And he told me that if I do this well   1900
I could keep the land forever free from pain.
Accordingly my pledge of all these things was heard
By the God and by all-seeing Zeus of the Oaths.
ANTIGONE
If these things have pleased him so,
They must suffice for us. But send us
To ancient Thebes, if by some means our journey there

Might hinder the imminent murder of our brothers.

THESEUS

I shall do this, and am prepared to do whatever else
May gratify both you and the man beneath the earth,
Who has just gone from us; and in such labour   1910
I must not cease.

CHORUS

Stop, raise no further lamentation.
For all these things are promised sovereign.

[*Exeunt omnes*

Abbreviations in these notes:

O.T.   *Oedipus the Tyrant*
O.C.   *Oedipus at Colonus*

NOTES TO ANTIGONE

1   (line 66) cf. Milton, *Paradise Lost* (1674), II, 465–6: 'This enterprise / None shall partake with me'.

2   (line 99) The First Choral Ode. This song expresses the relief of the Theban citizens at their recent victory over the Argives and Polyneices. As often in such Choral Odes, one of the themes is the danger of *hubris*, the arrogance by which extraordinary persons grasp for too much power, drawing the resentment and retribution of the Gods. The first stanza tells of an Argive leader who cried 'Victory!' too soon, and was punished for this *hubris* by the direct assault of Zeus' thunderbolt. As we hear or read this passage, we may look for hubristic behaviour among the principals: in Antigone perhaps, who defied the laws of the king, but more certainly in Creon, whose laws contradict those of the Gods (as Antigone points out in the second *Episode*).

Notes to the first stanza
the crashing noise of Ares: Ares is the War God, and his noise is that of battle.
clanging golden arms: here as in Aeschylus' play *The Seven Against Thebes*, the equipment of the Argive faction includes gold-decorated armour.
mad motions of the Bacchanal: the warrior's battle-frenzy is being compared to the religious possession experienced by the worshippers of Dionysus (also called Bacchus; cf. sixth chorus below). In the fourth stanza of the present Choral Song (and again later, in the sixth chorus) the Chorus will pray that they may be led by Bacchus himself in their celebration. Theorists of tragedy (including Friedrich Nietzsche in *The Birth of Tragedy from the Spirit of Music*) have proposed that its origin lay

in just such a ritual transfiguration of the citizen chorus-leader into the God. See Silk and Stern, *Nietzsche on Tragedy*.

3 (line 153) Jebb gives the following note here: 'There is a general dramatic analogy between this speech and that of Oedipus in O.T. 216–75. In each case a Theban king addresses Theban elders, announcing a stern decree, adopted in reliance on his own wisdom, and promulgated with haughty consciousness of power; the elders receive the decree with a submissive deference under which we can perceive traces of misgiving; and as the drama proceeds, the elders become spectators of calamities occasioned by the decree, while its author turns to them for comfort.' (Jebb, 40). Note also that Creon has been Regent of Thebes. With the sons of Oedipus now dead in the recent war, Creon has assumed the throne.

4 (line 203) For the vultures and dogs, see *Iliad*, 1, 4–5; for the list of the rebels' thwarted intentions, see Shakespeare, *Henry V*, 2, 2.

5 (line 411) The phrase 'good luck' translates the one word *hermaion*, 'gift of Hermes'.

6 (line 461) As the scholiast (the ancient commentator on the text) explains, this indicates that the speaker (the Guard) is a household slave of the extended family that includes both Creon and Antigone (Jebb, 87).

7 (line 509) Compare Haemon's speech to Creon below at 743–9; also see Sophocles' *Ajax*, 1250–4.

8 (line 595) The point here seems to be that Ismene is not willing to accept utter exclusion from either the crime or the punishment. Whereas Jebb took these *logoi* to be Ismene's protests, it seems to me even more logical to suppose that Ismene is insisting that her own influence was part of Antigone's decision, even if only as a foil or partner in debate. Ismene has given up trying to persuade Antigone to live, and is now trying to work out a way either to die with Antigone or to feel less isolated by Antigone's withdrawal from the world of the living, which has already begun (see lines following).

9 (line 835) Entombing the victim without providing any nourishment would incur *miasma*, the same kind of religious

pollution brought about by, for instance, the unavenged murder of Laius in O.T. Just as in that case, the pollution would befall the whole city of Thebes, not just its king. See note 17, below.

10 (line 848) cf. Keats, 'And when I feel, *fair creature of an hour!* / That I shall never look upon thee more,' from 'When I Have Fears That I May Cease To Be.'

11 (line 849) cf. the somewhat different 'Whom Gods destroy, they first make mad'; also Paul's *Epistle to the Hebrews* 12:6, 'Whom He loveth, He chasteneth.'

12 (line 859) That is, the same decree from which Haemon is swerving, namely Creon's current policy.

13 (line 878) Niobe is meant. She was Queen of Thebes by marriage to its King, Amphion. Niobe boasted that she had borne many children, whereas the Goddess Leto had borne only two, Artemis and Apollo. Those two Gods then destroyed all of Niobe's children. She returned to her home on Mt Sipylus, where her grief turned her to stone. Various ancient authors described a formation in the rockface that suggested a female figure, perpetually 'weeping' the rain; this was 'the Niobe of Sipylus'. cf. *Hamlet*, 1,2, 'Like Niobe, all tears'. Aeschylus and Sophocles each wrote a tragedy called *Niobe*; the plays are lost.

14 (line 887) Niobe was divine in that her father was a son of Zeus.

15 (line 910) The Labdacidae (or 'house of Labdacus') are descendants of Oedipus' grandfather, Labdacus. See the genealogy in this volume.

16 (line 920) By 'pious action' the Chorus refers to Antigone's religious burial of her brother.

17 (line 942) Here again, Creon is careful to point out that he will not directly kill Antigone. To do so would incur religious pollution (*miasma*) and the risk of divine punishment (*nemesis*). See note 9, above.

18 (line 953) This refers to Eteocles.

19 (line 1006) In the following Choral Ode, the powerlessness of mortal persons to resist their fates is evoked by a series of

exemplary stories that have in common *the imprisonment of a nobly-born person*. As Jebb points out, 'Danaë and Cleopatra were innocent; Lycurgus was guilty . . . the Chorus do not mean to shed light on Antigone's guilt or innocence . . . the ode is neutral, purely a free lyric treatment of the examples.' (Jebb, 168) Note: The famous Cleopatra VII (*c.*69BC–30BC), last Ptolemaic monarch of Egypt, is named for the mythical figure invoked in this ode.

20 (line 1015) This is Lycurgus, who vehemently opposed the worship of Dionysus when the latter arrived in Thrace. In retaliation, the God drove Lycurgus mad.

21 (line 1018) This archaic English spelling (*aweful*) of modern *awful* (attested, for instance, in John Florio's 1598 Italian-English Dictionary) better suggests the original sense of the word (i.e., full of that which inspires awe in the beholder), which better suits the Greek here.

22 (line 1022) *Bacchus* is an alternate name for Dionysus; he was worshipped by Maenads, women who achieved a kind of trance, swinging torches and sounding a now-untranslatable cry of 'euoi!' cf. the last lines of the first Choral Ode in *Oedipus the Tyrant*.

23 (line 1027) The Bosphorus (also called Bosporus) is the point where the Black Sea joins the Mediterranean (hence the phrase 'double sea'). An important trade and nautical route, it got its name from the myth of Io, who, having been transformed into a cow (*bous* in Greek), was pursued over much of the world's surface by a stinging fly, until she came here and crossed (*phoros* is derived from a Greek verb *pherein*, meaning carry or bring) the water. So, the Bosphorus is the water that 'carried the cow'. The Kyeneai are small, rocky islands in the Black Sea, just north of the Bosphorus; Salmydessus was near the Bosphorus on the northwest coast.

24 (line 1030) The sons of Phineus were blinded by their step-mother Eidothea. She was the sister of the hero Cadmus, from whom the Thebans claimed descent. cf. *Oedipus the Tyrant*, line 1.

25 (line 1041) Cleopatra's mother was Oreithyia, daughter of Erechtheus (a hero whose temple, the Erectheum, still stands

on the Athenian Acropolis). Boreas, the North Wind, seized Oreithyia and carried her off.

26 (line 1048) This is the same word order as the Greek, because this line is so brief and so pivotal (it's the question whose answer precipitates the climax and the outcome) that the order of the meanings as they emerge from Creon's mouth seems to me significant, over and above the grammatical fact that the Greek line would make the same sense no matter what the word order. But Sophocles has chosen this order: first interrogative, then address, and lastly the adverb '*now*'. One could say, 'Aged Teiresias, what is the news?' but this solution makes the Greek sequence of concepts disappear into an English idiom.

27 (line 1067) God of fire, and hence equivalent to fire itself. Agni is his (Hephaestus') Indic counterpart in Indo-European religious mythology. He too is sometimes presented as an articulate personage, and at other times as fire itself.

28 (line 1099) cf. O.T. 831

29 (line 1102) i.e. wizards, prophets, soothsayers.

30 (line 1119) Untranslatable exclamation, like the Yiddish *Oi* (which closely resembles, in form and function, another Greek exclamation, *oimoi*, with the slight difference that the second syllable of *oimoi* does have a semantic meaning, namely 'to/for me'; hence its conventional translation 'Ah, me' or 'woe is me'). Expresses frustration, dread, ruefulness, and the kind of self-pity of the English 'woe is me' or 'alas'.

31 (line 1139) Creon's suggestion is that Teiresias has been hired, by other Thebans (perhaps the Chorus), to convince Creon to permit the burial. As often in Sophocles (cf. Ismene at line 85 and Antigone's response), one character is reluctant to speak, until another insists that he or she do so, regardless of the consequences.

32 (line 1146) i.e. those of Antigone and Polyneices.

33 (line 1160) Sarcastic irony.

34 (line 1199) Semele was the daughter of Cadmus (legendary hero-king-founder of Thebes) and Harmonia. Zeus' love for Semele drew the jealous rage of Zeus' wife Hera, who tricked

the mortal woman into praying of Zeus that he come to her in the same undiminished form in which he would normally come to Hera. That theophany (god-appearance) included the thunderbolt aspect of Zeus, which immediately destroyed the human being. cf. line 1139. Also, see Ovid *Metamorphoses*, 3. 298. As Christopher Marlowe's *Doctor Faustus* praises Helen of Troy, he refers to this myth of Semele obliterated by the revealed Zeus/Jupiter:

> O thou art fairer then the euening aire,
> Clad in the beauty of a thousand starres,
> Brighter art thou then flaming *Iupiter*,
> When he appeard to haplesse *Semele* . . .

35   (line 1215) Jebb's note: 'The *kissos* [ivy] was to Dionysus what the *daphne* [laurel] was to Apollo. The crowning with ivy (*kissosis*) was a regular part of his festival.' Jebb, p. 202.

36   (line 1219) See note 22. Untranslatable ritual utterance shouted in the worship of Dionysus. We can attach no semantic meaning to this word, but its religious importance is great. For the possibility that the lack of a semantic meaning is part of the word's original nature, see the parallel argument about Sanskrit Mantras in Frits Stahl, *Ritual and Mantra: Rules Without Meaning*.

37   (line 1260) In Greek, the line runs: '*Haimon ololen: autocheir d' haimassetai*'. The first word (Haemon's name) and last word ('he bloodies') are both from a root meaning 'blood'. Also note that according to Jebb the word 'autocheir' is ambiguous, and can here mean either 'by his own hand' or 'by a kinsman's hand'.

38   (line 1291) Hecate, the wife of Pluto/Hades.

39   (line 1360) A circumlocution. Literally, 'if Themis should speak'. Meaning: *if it were within the purview of the Goddess of right custom (Themis) to say so*: i.e., 'so to speak,' 'if I may say so,' 'if you will'.

40   (line 1375) cf. O.T., 808–9, where Laius hits Oedipus 'meson kara' (in the middle of the head) from above, with the *kentron* or double-pointed horse-goad.

41   (line 1390) cf. 1030, Teiresias to Creon, 'What strength is this, to kill a corpse again?'

42   (line 1412) Megarius' and Haemon's, respectively.

43 (line 158) Pytho is another name for Delphi; its oracular shrine is therefore called the Pythia, as is the priestess who served there as the mouthpiece of Apollo. Pythia is 'golden' because of the vast stores of wealth accumulated there through decades of pilgrimage and votive giving, as well as the temporarily deposited accounts awaiting eventual withdrawal (see Jebb 1893, p. 31). Apollo is called Healer in his capacity as a divine sponsor of medicine; he was born on the sacred island of Delos, hence 'Delian'.

44 (line 176) This is worse than an infertility curse in which nobody can get pregnant; here, those who are pregnant and due to deliver find themselves unable to do so. Plato further developed this idea in the *Symposium*: 'When what is pregnant comes near to beauty, whatever is pregnant becomes gracious, and pours itself forth, delighted, and gives birth and procreates. Whereas amid what is ugly, it broods and is distressed, and shrinks back and turns away and is repulsed, and doesn't give birth, so the pregnancy is very difficult to bear.' (206d5–d7)

45 (line 199) See note 22.

46 (line 307) The 'Ode on Man' in the *Antigone* ('Marvels are many . . .') celebrates human understanding for its sublime use-value. Teiresias' terrible understanding is not human (since he only has it as the prophet of Apollo, who shares divine knowledge with him), nor is it useful: the failures of Laius and Oedipus to elude fulfilment of Apollo's pronouncements is evidence of just how useless divine knowledge must be for human beings. In *Oedipus Tyrannus: Lame Knowledge and the Homosporic Womb,* John Hay observes that a century after Sophocles, Aristotle claims in the first sentence of the *Metaphysics* that 'all human beings by their nature desire to know'; Teiresias' attitude, therefore, is supernatural not only in his knowledge of a future that only the Gods can foresee, but also in his revulsion from such knowing.

47 (line 372) 'Hikanos Apollon' can be understood to mean 'Apollo is capable' or 'Apollo is sufficient.' The first reading is

a truism; it goes without saying that the God is capable of destroying the man. But the second reading reaches much deeper into tragedy's intractable philosophical problems.

48 (line 393) The verb for 'hitting the mark' is *tungkhano*; its opposite is *hamartano*, to 'miss the mark'. The noun form is *hamartia*, Aristotle's word for the 'mistake' that undoes the tragic hero. Toward the end of this quarrel, Teiresias will turn Oedipus' archery-metaphor against him.

49 (line 679) This reading departs from Jebb in favour of the Scholiast (i.e. it agrees with an ancient commentator rather than with Sir Richard Claverhouse Jebb, the great Victorian classicist without whose work much of modern scholarship on Sophocles would be impossible). Since the Chorus represents the collective Theban citizenry and, in effect, the Athenian audience (see Vernant, 1990), there may be a rich vein of Sophoclean irony here: Creon is known to 'these here' as the irrational and hubristic tyrant of the *Antigone* drama from twelve years back, whereas this scene shows him sane and satiated. Oedipus is in the same state of royally hubristic blindness that we know will afflict Creon in the narrative future, because we have already seen that later episode in an earlier festival.

50 (line 866) Calculating seems like the most reliable tool for rational mastery of an irrational world, and mathematical propositions like this one are among the foundations of our understanding. Yet the moment of Oedipus' greatest triumph, the solving of the Sphinx's riddle, was also a moment of mathematical paradox in which one creature (man) seemed to have many different bodies (each with a different number of legs); one leg (the lower limbs of the infant Oedipus, pinned together with a stake) became many (two lame legs and a cane); and one man (Oedipus, who answered the riddle) became the equal of many men (everyman, to whom the riddle accurately applies). Also, the doctrine of sovereignty espoused in the drama's opening scene includes the idea that the pain of all comes into one, which gets frighteningly inverted in images of an empty city whose only inhabitant is a king with no subjects except himself (O.T. 54–7; Ant. 739). And the ironies

of these lines are inexhaustible: 'Clearly then, it was not I who killed him./For one and many cannot be made equal' also encapsulates the larger issue of sacrifice and collective purification through the exile of a scapegoat. The one and the many are to some degree conflated in punishment, since 'the whole people sickens' of the plague, and in responsibility, since as Jocasta says at O.T. 981, 'already in their dreams have many mortals/Lain down with their mothers.' Finally (for the purposes of this note), the effect of Apollo's curse is to make what should have been more-than-one (a husband entering Jocasta's body sexually, and a son leaving it obstetrically) into one (Oedipus the son-husband).

51 (line 1011) Jocasta has been reassuring Oedipus as he worries over the incest prophecy; here, Oedipus responds that her reassurances would be very useful if his mother (i.e. Merope) were not alive. Oedipus is referring to the reassuring remarks (on mother-incest) spoken *by* Jocasta, but the construction (in the translation and, I think, in the Greek) implies an incestuous subtext in which the remarks on mother-incest are also spoken *about* Jocasta. In this English construction, 'of' introduces the agent after a passive verb. Jebb employs it in rendering O.T. 816, 'what mortal could prove more hated of Heaven?' Common in Shakespeare, it is amply evidenced ;in the O.E.D.'s article on 'of', part V, entry 15. In the Greek, the pronoun indicating Jocasta is in the dative case with the pluperfect passive verb of speaking, indicating that she is the speaker. But the audience is enduring the exquisite irony of Jocasta's discussing this issue using the word mother and Oedipus responding as he does. That irony arises because Jocasta and Oedipus think they are discussing Merope while in fact they are discussing Jocasta. Her lines are spoken 'by' her, and, in the modern sense, 'of' her.

52 (line 64) The 'brazen threshold' is a bronze stairway leading into a deep ravine thought to issue into the underworld. Oedipus will disappear into it upon his exit near the end of the play.

53 (line 113) According to Jebb, the libation peculiar to the Eumenides was unusual in this regard, being a mixture of honey, milk, and water.

54 (line 177) This metaphoric equivalent of 'what is one to think' is consistent with the Greek usage whereby, in Aristotle's *Rhetoric*, the orator goes to various 'topics' – literally, 'places' – in rhetorical space in order to fill out the speech. Similarly in English idiom, to speak on an issue is 'to take a position'.

55 (line 210) i.e. guiding Oedipus, as the Chorus is now doing.

56 (line 253) i.e. the need for purification from pollution which Oedipus' presence in the grove might incur.

57 (line 309) cf. O.T. 461, Teiresias to Oedipus: 'Go into these affairs, and reckon them.' The verb there is *logizou* and the emphasis is on Oedipus' reliance on his own mind. Here the verb is *dia-eidenai*, and the idea is that Theseus, when he comes, will come to a thorough knowledge of the situation.

58 (line 311) A *xenos* is a foreigner, a stranger, a guest, or, as in this case, a host. The institution of guest-host relationship and hospitality is called *xenia*.

59 (line 329) cf. O.T. 217–8, Oedipus of himself, the criminal: 'By himself, himself accusing.' Oedipus is a noble man who was his own mutilator. But from the perspective of his holy maturity in O.C., that self-wounding was an act of nurturance and self-care: it saved his moral life. The present expression 'what noble man is not his own friend' is true and untrue of Oedipus in the same way that the riddle of the Sphinx does and does not apply to him (he was lame all his life and therefore walked on three legs in the afternoon, when the riddle requires two).

60 (line 340) cf. O.T. 79–80, Oedipus of the approaching Creon: 'May he come brilliant in fortune, With a bright face to bring salvation.'

61 (line 440) The old sense of 'virtue,' *power* (as in *the virtue of an elixir*) is intended.

62 (line 458) Ismene responds to Oedipus' last verb, forgetting the grammar of his first. This happens occasionally in Greek.

63 (line 525) cf. O.T. 101: Oedipus: 'And what cleansing?'

64 (line 566) Just after this phrase, *huphegettoi dicha* 'second guide,' the speech prefix 'Ismene' follows. The subtext seems to be that Ismene is *not* Oedipus' second guide; he has Antigone and no other.

65 (line 583) Untranslatable exclamation, approximating to 'woe is me'.

66 (line 585) Untranslatable exclamation, approximating to Hamlet's 'fie upon't! Oh, fie!'

67 (line 667) If Theseus grants Oedipus eventual burial in Athens, he will also protect Oedipus from Creon's imminent attempt to coerce him to the Theban side in the meantime.

68 (line 689) cf. O.T. circa 849: 'And wouldn't one be right, to judge That all this came upon me from a spirit, Cruel, and beyond the things of man?'

69 (line 698) Lewis Campbell and Evelyn Abbott give: 'Because it is their fate to be overthrown in this land.' See their Oxford school edition of 1878, p. 81 (note to line 605).

70 (line 739) Jebb (taking *sunoisomai* slightly differently) gives: 'thy will shall be mine,' recalling Dante, *Inferno* 2, 139: *Or va, ch'un sol volere e d'ambedue,* 'Now go, for but one will is in the pair of us.' This is called heteronomy (as opposed to autonomy).

71 (line 753) cf. Shakespeare, *Julius Caesar*, 2, 1, 129: 'Swear priests and cowards and men cautelous . . . unto bad causes swear Such creatures as men doubt.' The point is that with a good man, oaths are unnecessary.

72 (line 789) Demeter and her daughter Persephone, who plucked the narcissus as she was seized by Hades.

73 (line 795) According to Pausanias 1, 30, 2, there were altars to the Muses, to Hermes, and to Athena here.

74   (line 848) i.e. Antigone, upon whom Creon himself eventually
      inflicts the suffering unto death, in the drama called *Antigone*
      which constitutes the sequel to the *Oedipus at Colonus* though
      Sophocles had presented it forty years earlier, in around 441.
      Thus the horrible irony in Creon's present remark can only be
      available to the audience, not the characters, since for them
      Antigone's dismal end is the unknowable future; the audience
      knows all about it.

75   (line 858) i.e. Athens.

76   (line 876) *Sklera malthakōs legōn*. This has several layers of
      metaphoricity. As Jebb's note explains, Creon is 'disguising the
      ungenerous treatment which was really contemplated (399)
      under the name of a recall to home and friends (757).' In
      Ancient Greek as in English, the 'hard' is the physically
      conservative object that isn't easily changed; and by way of this
      literal meaning, a metaphoric one develops, where the hard is
      'the difficult', with or without any literally hard object. Also,
      this figure of speech bears a sexual overtone derivable from
      the association between violent aggression and male sexual
      arousal; the suggestion is that Creon's seduction of Oedipus
      back toward Thebes (the scene of incest, and the memory of
      parricide) amounts to a hubristic violation. See Sigmund Freud;
      René Girard; Herbert Marcuse; also David Cohen, *Law,
      Sexuality and Society in Ancient Athens*, and the literature on
      Dionysus, Priapus, and Athenian cockfighting.

77   (line 877) *Akontas philein*. 'unwilling [to] love'. I defer to
      Jebb, who insists that this refers to *Oedipus'* refusal (*akontas*) of
      Creon's apparent loving kindness (*philein*), not to *Creon's* gift
      of kindness (*philein*) under constraint (*akontas*) by the oracle
      demanding the return to Thebes of Oedipus' body. However
      we construct the grammar, the line contains an implicit
      critique of all the filiative relationships that have proven so
      disastrous for him: the love of families for their members is,
      like Oedipus' parricide and incest, *akontas*, unwilled, not
      chosen.

78   (line 893) cf. *Hamlet*, 4, 4, 64–5, 'not tomb enough and continent
      to hide the slain.' Jebb notes *I Henry IV*, 5, 4, 89.

79 (line 899) cf. *Hamlet*, 3,4, 'these words like daggers enter in mine ears.'

80 (line 924) The Athenians, impartial judges.

81 (line 927) The Athenians, and their king, Theseus.

82 (line 965) This is either Creon ordering one of his guards to seize Antigone and leave with her, or Creon vying with the Chorus; I favour the latter.

83 (line 969) Although unmarked in the Greek repetition of '*O xenoi, xenoi*', I understand a possible modulation here among the ranges of meaning for the word *xenos*. The crisis onstage at this point is the breakdown of *xenia*, the demands of hospitality which govern the relations among *xenoi* (who are guests or hosts or strangers or foreigners).

84 (line 984) e.g. Oedipus' conflicts with Laius (O.T. 807); Teiresias (O.T. 345); Creon (O.T. 583); Jocasta (O.T. 1067); and himself (O.T. 1268).

85 (line 1044) i.e. as fast as possible (not restraining the horse).

86 (line 1099) The Areopagus (which Sophocles names here in a *tmesis*, splitting the name into its two parts, 'pagos' and 'Areos') was the ancient, aristocratically controlled civic-religious court of Athens. Its powers, though eventually circumscribed by the reforms of Pericles and Ephialtes, seem to have persisted in this kind of case (i.e. the expulsion of undesirables).

87 (line 1103) In fact Oedipus cursed Creon only *after* Creon began to set upon Oedipus.

88 (line 1107) Jebb notes Sophocles' *Electra*, 1170, 'I do not see the dead suffering'; Campbell and Abbot (1878) note *Macbeth*, 3, 2, 'Duncan is in his grave; After life's fitful fever he sleeps well; Treason has done his worst; nor steel, nor poison, Malice domestic, foreign levy, nothing, Can touch him further.' They also note Aeschylus fragment 250, 'No pain touches the dead.' See also Job 3: 13–9. The action of the next drama in the narrative, *Antigone*, proves Creon disastrously wrong about crucial questions surrounding this very issue.

89 (line 1117) This is a deeply Greek idea and the focus of Plato's *Euthyphro,* in which Socrates asks the question: 'Is the holy

holy because the gods love it, or do the gods love it because it
is holy?' If the former, then anything the divine chooses must
be regarded as, somehow, right – for instance, Oedipus' incest,
parricide, and mutilation ('Apollo is enough'; 'It was Apollo,
O my friends'), or Abraham's near-killing of his son Isaac at
God's behest. But if the gods love what is holy because it
already possesses an inherent holiness, then theism is in trouble
('Religion limps away').

90 (line 1122) *Epei didaxon.* This is what grammarians call 'the
controversial *epei*', a favourite idiom of Oedipus, as at O.T.
385: *epei, pher' eipe*: 'or if not, come, explain.'

91 (line 1129) This verb (*phaino*) means show or appear, or be
exposed, or, idiomatically, be born. Oedipus is referring to his
birth (which is wretched because of what the oracles foretell),
but indirectly to the self-exposure of his guilt in O.T., and to
Creon's denouncing him in the speech to which he now
responds.

92 (line 1168) Line 1009 runs: *auton t'echeirou tas koras t' oichei
labwn.* Jebb renders 'and did seek to seize me, and hast already
carried off my daughters.' This allows for the fact that Creon,
who would manhandle (*echeirou*, 'seize by hands') Oedipus, has
apparently 'taken away' the daughters only through his henchmen (who recently captured the daughters and brought them
to Thebes). Still, *oichei* is a second person singular and its subject
is Creon. Oedipus has already used this same idiom at 895.

93 (line 1207) The emphasis on sacred geography makes this Choral Ode difficult. The first stanza expresses the Chorus' wish to
witness a possible fight between the fleeing Thebans (who hold
Oedipus' daughters) and their Athenian pursuers. The fight
might happen at the torch-lit coast, in the Bay of Eleusis (the
torches are part of the Eleusinian Mysteries, one of whose
religious functions is a tending to the souls of the dead), or at
the site of the Pythian temple of Apollo, at a point some five
miles distant on the coast of the same Bay. The 'Goddesses' are
here not the Eumenides, but Demeter and Persephone, whose
Mystery rites were performed at Eleusis. The Eumolpidae were
a genealogical group whose office in the Eleusinian Mysteries
involved keeping the rites secret.

94 (line 1325) *Ouk ogkos*. 'Of no great importance' can also mean, through a homophone, 'not full of barbs.' In fact, the speech will be both: important and barbed.

95 (line 1461) i.e. those of the curse on the family of Labdacus, Oedipus' grandfather, which includes all his descendants.

96 (line 1464) The Peloponnese, a land formation in the Aegean and the isthmus by which it connects to the rest of mainland Greece. It has many names, derived from a variety of mythological figures including Pelops and Apis. Argos, like the rest of the Peloponnese, is Doric because at some point early in the Archaic Period a Hellenic people called the Dorians migrated/ invaded southward into the Peloponnese and remained there, founding Spartan culture. Also, Sophocles is making it clear that he refers to Doric Argos and not to any other cities of that name elsewhere.

97 (line 1482) This list of the seven captains derives from Aeschylus' play, *Seven Against Thebes*. Readers of Homer's *Iliad* will recognise that this generation preceded that of the Trojan War; e.g. Tydeus was the father of Diomedes.

98 (line 1505) i.e. Theseus, who sent Polyneices to Oedipus from Poseidon's altar, where Polyneices had been found.

99 (line 1531) The *daimon* is to be understood as something demonic, because divine and alive, but also something conceptual, like fate or a curse.

100 (line 1553) 'Stygian' means 'hateful,' apropos of another related piece of infernal geography, the river Styx. Tartarus is a region of the underworld; Erebus is the darkness thereof, and in some texts it seems to be a kind of equivalent to Tartarus, or to denote another portion of the underworld. The darkness of hell is here called 'paternal'. Jebb gives much interesting speculation on this (e.g. it could mean a darkness that is father to everything; or darkness like that experienced by Polyneices' blind father, Oedipus; or the darkness of Oedipus' own father Laius, who is already in Tartarus; or the darkness peculiar to a father's curse.) Campbell and Abbott take this last, citing *King Lear*, 1, 1, where a father wishes his daughter 'dowered with our curse'. Note also that Oedipus has just spat Polyneices out like spittle, in the same utterance as he disowned him; this

suggests a reduction of paternity to the sexual mechanics that produced it (as the *Koran* often points out, 'man is a bit of cast-off semen').

101 (line 1591) 'Yes, for he wishes it' refers to Oedipus; 'But I must not give in,' apparently refers to Eteocles. The beauty of this is that by insisting upon his need to fight Eteocles, Polyneices is giving in precisely to the wish of Oedipus.

102 (line 1603) The Greek idiom here is roughly 'you will never see me seeing again'; because when next they see him he will be dead. This idiom, so frequently employed by the heroine of *Antigone*, suggests that being able to look on the light of day is a salient characteristic of the living, which in turn suggests the self-annihilating aspect of Oedipus' self-blinding in the *Oedipus Tyrannus*.

103 (line 1633) cf. *Hamlet*, I, I, 116–28. 'A little ere the mightiest Julius fell . . . disasters in the sun . . . And prologue to the omen coming on.'

104 (line 1721) i.e. Cerberus, the three-headed dog that guards the Underworld.

105 (line 1739) Jebb's note: 'The rift or cavern at Colonus, from which the adjoining region took the name of *chalkous hodos* ('the bronze road'), was locally supposed to be connected to the 'brazen threshold' below by brazen steps reaching down into the underworld.'

106 (line 1743) Peirithous and Theseus had made a trip to Hades, their cooperation guaranteed by a sacrifice at this spot. 'Thoricus' was an Attic *deme* (that is, one of the pseudo-genealogical groups established by Athenian political reforms for the diffusion of political factions). These details of local geography are less important than their function as landmarks: Oedipus died at such and such a spot.

107 (line 1820) While this is certainly the main idea of the Greek *bebēken* when it stands alone (as it does here), its literal sense is closer to 'has he stepped / left by walking.'

108 (line 1850) The Greek here is difficult. Jebb sees Antigone wishing she had had an opportunity to perform the office of burial (which we associate with her because of her burial of

Polyneices in the *Antigone*, an earlier play about later events). Ismene's answering remark evokes the ending of the *Oedipus Tyrannus*, in which Oedipus describes the future predicament of his daughters, and the opening lines of the *Antigone*, in which the daughters discuss their predicament.

109 (line 1890) Nemesis is the retaliation of the Gods. Theseus' point is that the holy circumstances of Oedipus' death, the oracles surrounding it, and the dead man's compact with Theseus, together constitute a mutually beneficial arrangement in which the Gods below are involved, so that further grief implies a slight against them and a doubt about all the proposed benefits (Oedipus' painless death, his protection of Athens with his secret tomb at Colonus, and perhaps even Theseus' promise to protect the daughters).